Mary Mortimer was born in Au[...]
Indonesian, French and Educati[...]
has been married three times an[...]
Rachel, from her first marriage. [...]
1979; Jack, her second husband, [...]

Mary Mortimer is a teacher and librarian, and author of *Boys Do, Girls Are*; several articles about sex stereotyping; as well as co-author of *CatSkill*, an interactive multi-media library training package; and contributor to *Willing to Listen, Wanting to Die*. She currently teaches at the Canberra Institute of Technology.

MARY MORTIMER

When Your
Partner
Dies

First published in Great Britain by The Women's Press Ltd, 1995
A member of the Namara Group
34 Great Sutton Street, London EC1V 0DX

Copyright © Mary Mortimer 1991, 1995

The right of Mary Mortimer to be identified as the author of this work has been asserted by her in accordance with the Copyright, Designs and Patents Act 1988.

British Library Cataloguing-in-Publication Data
A catalogue record for this book is available from the British Library

ISBN 0 7043 4390 8

Phototypeset in Sabon & Franklin Gothic by Intype, London
Printed and bound in Great Britain by BPC Paperbacks Ltd, Aylesbury

Dedication

To my parents, Joyce and Ray, whose unfailing love and support carried me through terrible loneliness and despair.

And

To my children, Michael and Rachel, for whom the struggle always seemed necessary and worthwhile, and who amazed me by their understanding and maturity when I needed them most.

Contents

In Memoriam

These people are remembered in the writing of this book. Their families helped me to sort out and to understand the experiences we shared. Those who have died and those who survive them have all contributed to a warmer and deeper understanding of the significance of loss.

John Charles Julius Johnston	2 April 1907 – 24 January 1975
Rex Alfred Mortimer	11 February 1926 – 31 December 1979
Maryan Huntsman	6 June 1962 – 26 June 1985
Norman Stanley McAsey	25 April 1923 – 17 December 1986
Raymond John (Jack) Meredith	4 July 1935 – 8 July 1987
Betty Merle McAsey	22 July 1928 – 14 December 1987
Pamela Bavin Denoon	6 March 1942 – 17 September 1988

Acknowledgements

Writing this book has been painful and liberating. I have depended heavily on the encouragement of my friends, especially Pamela and Donald Denoon, Nadine Meredith, Leone and Bob Huntsman, Jeni Black, Amirah and Ken Inglis, Andrew Gonczi and Roz Gatwood, Rita Nash, Helen Kerr-Rourbicek, Hilda Gray, Beverley Kemp, John Morrison and Ruby Tinker.

My understanding of what I was going through was enormously enhanced by Julie Dunsmore, my grief counsellor, who 'put me back together' on many occasions when I was falling apart. She also helped hugely in the writing of this book, since she was able to remind me of the difficult and ambivalent feelings I had 'forgotten' after I worked my way through them.

I am grateful to Marilyn Barnett of Clapham & Collinge, John Oliver of the Voluntary Euthanasia Society, Mr Geoff May of the National Association of Funeral Directors, the helpful young man in the Department of Social Security, Avril Jackson of the Hospice Information Service, the Cremation Society of Great Britain, Cruse Bereavement Care, Revd Whelan of the Whittington Hospital, the National Council for Voluntary Organisations, and the London office of the Registrar of Births, Deaths and Marriages for their information and advice; Joan Braybrook for making many enquiries and for her 'local knowledge'; Jennifer Lewis for her ideas about the book's design; and Rebecca Sidoli for the verse 'When I am gone'.

Many friends and family members made valuable suggestions, including Jeni Black, Jon Clarke, Joyce Clarke, Colin Gray, Dennis Heffernan, Leone Huntsman, Amirah Inglis, Stephen Johnston and Margaret Watkinson, Jenny McAsey, Nadine Meredith and Claire O'Conor.

The belief Sylvia Hale and Heather Cam have shown in the book cheered and encouraged me greatly. Kathy Gale's enthusiasm has brought about the British edition.

I might not have persevered to publication without the untiring encouragement and support of Donald Denoon, whose editing and good humour have undoubtedly improved the quality of the book and my mood while writing it.

Finally, my thanks to all those with whom I have talked about my experiences and my feelings. Without their willing participation, I could not have clarified my thoughts well enough to put them into writing.

Preface

I have written this book in an attempt to make sense of the two major tragedies in my life – the deaths of two partners, each of whom I loved deeply. These deaths, and that of a dear friend, are my main personal experiences of bereavement. I have therefore focused on the death of a partner, although I am strongly aware of the devastation which can result from the death of a parent or a child.

When we lose a parent, and especially both parents, we lose the generation 'above' us, the source of our life, our early knowledge of the world, so many of our characteristics and attitudes. Even if our parents are old and infirm, and have begun to lose their authority before they die, their death marks a final, irrevocable change in our status: we are children no longer, and that adds powerfully to our grief at the loss of a loved one.

When our child dies, at whatever age, we are stunned by the unnatural order of events. We do not expect to survive our children: our hopes are for their future, even more than our own.

With the death of a partner, on the other hand, we lose the person who shares our everyday life, who is there for breakfast and dinner, with whom we share a home, a bed, many of our hopes and fears, memories and future plans. So the loss affects every aspect of our lives, and requires the most pervasive practical and emotional adjustments to the way we live.

There are other books which present a more academic

or professional approach to bereavement. I have written from my own experience – and that of close friends whose grief I have shared. I have been able to draw conclusions about the common aspects of grieving, and the different effects of sudden and of expected death. I try to offer practical suggestions for dealing with situations you may not yet have encountered.

The book is drawn from my experience, which has been of heterosexual partnerships. However, losing a loved gay or lesbian partner is no less traumatic. Since the tragedy of the AIDS epidemic has struck the gay community with particular force, many people have experienced multiple losses, and they have had to find enormous strength and warmth to support their friends and partners. I hope this book will be helpful to all those who experience loss.

I grew up in Australia, in a predominantly Anglo-Celtic, Christian community. The experience of rituals of death and funerals which I describe is therefore quite personal, and may differ from other religions and communities. The civil requirements for dealing with death are general within the United Kingdom; unfortunately I am unable to detail customs within communities other than my own.

Since I am a very practical person, and control over my life is of great importance to me, I emphasise what can be *done* in coping with the loss of a partner and its aftermath. You may find it easier than I did to let things happen, to accept this massive disruption to your physical and emotional life. I hope, however, that you will find my descriptions of events and feelings reassuring and helpful. One of our most valuable sources of support in times of crisis is the knowledge that our experience is not unique, and that others have felt or behaved in a similar way.

Although I address those who have lost or are losing a partner, I hope that others will also read this book.

For most couples who are still together, one will have to live through and beyond the death of the other. Yet death is perhaps the last remaining taboo. Not only do we not talk about it, we don't even call it by name. We prefer to say that 'the deceased' or the 'dearly departed' or the 'loved one' has 'passed away', 'gone', 'left us', 'gone to Heaven', is 'at rest' or 'at peace'; we talk around the event without using the words. By not naming death and dying, we deny the reality and make it more difficult for those who are close to it to share and express their sadness, their anxiety and their anger.

This is equally so whether one is dying or watching a loved one die or grieving over the death of a loved one. This was especially true for me when my first husband was dying. I needed to talk about practical matters, especially the funeral arrangements. It seemed sensible (and it was!) to do what I could before he died, but I embarrassed some of my friends by raising the subject. What bad taste! they seemed to think; perhaps they even felt that somehow I was precipitating his end. But if I was going through the dying of my partner and my children's father, surely they could listen and not be shocked?

Many people who have no personal experience of death and loss, feel inadequate when a friend is bereaved. In their embarrassment they try to ignore this momentous event, and in so doing they add to their friend's feelings of hurt and isolation. In reading of my experiences, you may better understand your friend's suffering, and respond more confidently to their needs.

If you believe in a God or gods, and a life after death, I am sure it can be a great source of comfort and strength. I hope you do not turn away from your belief in your anger and feeling of betrayal. 'Why me?' is a very common reaction to tragedy. Though I do not believe in God or Heaven, I do have great faith in humankind: in our capacity to love and help each other, to share and give meaning to our joys and our sorrows. When I have felt most desolate, I have often asked 'Why me?' Perhaps part of the answer lies in this book.

1

Introduction

Until my first husband, Rex Mortimer, learned that he had cancer in August 1979, I had little experience of significant loss.

Dad

Even my father's death, in January 1975, was not too painful: we had not been especially close, but were on friendly terms and had no obvious unfinished business. He suffered from emphysema, and was tired of his increasingly confined existence. In our long talks we shared what we felt needed to be said. I was not greatly distressed by his death, except for the way it happened, which I discuss in 'Helping to Die'.

Rex

Rex's approaching death, however, was shattering. We had two children, Michael, aged nine, and Rachel, aged seven. Rex was a highly intelligent and thoughtful maverick. He had a fine sense of fun and found status and pomp ridiculous. He was committed to understanding and improving human conditions. He was much older than me, and had clear ideas about what he wanted to do with his life, yet he was open to my ideas and different approaches to living. Sometimes reluctantly at first, he adjusted to each new venture in our lives cheerfully and tolerantly. He was a devoted father, who had wanted children for a long time (he was 44 when Michael was born), and fully shared the responsibilities of parenting. He was happy for me to lead a fairly independent life in my work and with my own circle of friends, yet we also shared friends, and political and social attitudes and concerns. There were tensions, of course, about the burdens of the household, and how much independence we each sacrificed to the family. But by and large we were able to resolve our differences and live happily.

Then our world fell apart: active and irreversible cancer was diagnosed. Rex died in December of the same year. The children and I were left to pick up the pieces and make a new life for ourselves.

Jack

Not long after Rex's death I met Jack Meredith. He was recently divorced and, like me, looking for 'a fling' to make him feel alive again. Neither of us wanted or anticipated a committed relationship. We shared many attitudes, however, and were allies in a dramatic confrontation at work. Almost despite ourselves, we fell in love. His children were nearly independent, and he agonised about sharing responsibility for mine. I was ambivalent about giving up the independence I had begun to enjoy: making my own decisions, especially about the children; never having to compromise or take account of the needs or opinions of another adult. Yet the intensity of our passion and our need to share our lives with another adult, to laugh at the same jokes, to support each other, to go to concerts and plays together, to make love and feel newly and excitingly attractive, overcame our hesitations. Soon we were living together.

Jack was intense, and gave himself totally to everything he did. He became frustrated when his heart condition limited his ability to do all the things he wanted

to do. In recent years he had spent time usefully review-
ing his life, and gaining a better understanding of himself. If occasionally he was depressed or short-tempered,
mostly he was warm and supportive, understanding and
enthusiastic, living life to the full.

Then in July 1987, almost without warning, the
symptoms of impending heart attack re-appeared. He
admitted himself to hospital for tests, and two days later,
after another heart attack, and despite the expertise of
the intensive care unit, he died. The children were 16
and 14.

Events allowed me some time to get used to the idea
that Rex was going to die. For all the anguish of living
with that knowledge, and seeing one you love fade
before your eyes, it does at least prepare you somewhat
for the shock of the final separation. I had regarded
myself as unlucky to be widowed at 35, but felt that I
had put it behind me, and made a new and happy life
for myself and my children. When Jack died suddenly, I
was devastated. To experience such a loss again,
especially as I knew what lay ahead for all of us, was
shattering and unfair.

Pamela

My close friend Pamela Denoon learned that she had
leukaemia in November 1986. She resolved to understand and resist the disease – through natural diet, meditation, informing herself about available treatments and
their effects. She remained well for over a year, and we
all hoped for a miracle. But it didn't happen, and by
July 1988 she had entered the acute stage of the disease.
She died in September 1988.

Through all of this, my children, now teenagers, tried
to live 'ordinary lives'. But what confidence could they

have in a secure and happy future, without the continual
fear of losing those they love and depend upon? How
much tragedy could they endure, without serious cost to
their emotional well-being? The answer appears to be:
a great deal, provided they (and we) have a sufficiently
loving and supporting circle of family and friends, and
are enabled to work through our grief in a compassionate environment. No one would choose to endure my
family's losses of the last few years, but I believe we
have all been sensitised and strengthened by them.

2

Grief

Accepting and acknowledging your grief are necessary aspects of coming to terms with your loss. Grief encompasses a range of emotions – anger, sadness, loneliness, fear, guilt and helplessness. These emotions are all difficult, painful and negative, and it is tempting for us to believe we can choose not to experience them – or at least push them away as soon as we can. But to deny our feelings, especially such powerful ones, is simply to bury them inside ourselves, where they will continue to ache, and make us feel unhappy and depressed. Worse, they may fester, and sooner or later some minor incident will trigger an explosion of unresolved grief. The contrast between the trivial incident and the dramatic reaction is difficult to comprehend and makes us feel silly. Or we will feel angry and knotted inside, limiting our ability to love and trust again – that is, our ability to live emotionally full and satisfying lives.

Feelings

Everyone experiences grief differently, both the intensity of feeling and how long it takes before the loss of the partner (parent, child, relative, friend) is accepted. But the feelings are universal, and they can be shared with others who have lost someone close, or who suffer the same loss.

My bond with Jack's daughter, strong while he was alive, became unshakeable after his death. Fortunately

5

for us, we were both able to identify and openly discuss our feelings, so we shared our sense of irreplaceable loss, our desperate loneliness, our difficulties in concentrating on anything, the emptiness of all our activities, now that we could no longer share them with him. So we were able to support and encourage each other (not with trite promises of hope for the future – neither of us felt much like that), but with the warmth and understanding of genuine feeling for the other's pain.

Many people can provide this understanding and support. It is perhaps easiest for those who have experienced loss themselves. (Remember that loss is not only the result of death – a divorced friend will recognise the pain of a dreamed-of future no longer to be shared; loss of a job can produce a strong sense of disorientation and loss.) Your friends who love you and are willing to listen, to share with you their feelings and their memories, to bear your suffering with you, can all help you to cope.

When a friend's wife was dying, people worried about how he was coping emotionally. He seemed strong and in control; they asked each other how he really was, but seemed reluctant to ask him. When I did, he talked freely and openly, sharing his hopes and little triumphs as well as his pain. Why were others reluctant to ask him? Perhaps they were afraid to puncture his self-control, or felt that they might be overwhelmed by a full response: and they might not be able to share the burden of his suffering anyway. But we will all suffer loss in our lives, all feel helpless and hopeless and racked with emotional pain. The least we can do for ourselves and for others is to acknowledge and share, openly and caringly, the reality of sadness, despair, anger and loneliness, and help each other to grieve.

Physical Reactions

Although we anticipate our feelings of grief, we are often surprised by our physical responses. These include aches in the stomach or chest, unexpected fear or panic attacks, even urgent sexual need at times which seem totally inappropriate.

The night Rex died, when I finally stumbled home in the early hours, I went to bed and lay awake till morning. I was astonished to feel, along with everything else, intense sexual need. It felt odd and embarrassing, but it is quite a common physical response to grief.

After Jack died, I often felt a deep ache in my lower chest. Perhaps this is what the poets mean when they say you can 'feel your heart breaking'; it didn't feel very poetic – just painful and weakening.

Many people experience attacks of panic, which seem irrational. You may feel well enough to go shopping, only to find half-way round the supermarket that you have to get out, suddenly panic-stricken. It may be a good idea to go with a friend who can finish the shopping for you if necessary.

A few months after Jack died, I went to stay with an old friend who was getting married – a difficult occasion emotionally, when everyone else was celebrating the couple's love and future happiness, and I felt that mine had just been snatched away. We went shopping with her teenage son. In a card shop I saw the stationery Jack and I had bought together in Florence. I was in the queue with my cards and money when I was suddenly overwhelmed. Pushing the cards and money into the teenager's hands, I rushed from the shop and collapsed on to a seat in the arcade, sobbing wildly. My friend's bewildered son bought my cards, and understood what had happened when it was explained to him, but for me it was an embarrassing and frustrating loss of control.

If you are used to being competent and getting things done, it will frustrate you terribly to lose much of your ability. It is temporary, but for a while you may not be able to function as efficiently as you did before. I couldn't even read anything at all complicated – my brain seemed to have slowed down along with the rest of me.

As with fatigue (see also 'Fatigue'), I think you have to accept your physical responses, and not try to resist them. You *will* have more energy, you will feel more capable, as you begin to come to terms with your loss. Until then, be kind and forgiving to yourself. Your body will heal gradually as your heart does.

Grief Counselling

You may like a professional shoulder to lean on. In my experience support from a grief counsellor can be invaluable for you and your family. When Rex died, a friend suggested a bereavement counsellor, but I was proud and confident of my ability to handle my loss on my own. Of course I wasn't able to: I wore down many friends re-living and re-telling the events before and after his death; spilling out my anger and frustration to whoever would listen.

However compassionate your friends and family, your grief will be more profound and longer-lived than theirs. There will probably come a day when you are still lonely and hurting, but you feel you cannot expect them to go on listening to your sorrow, understanding your depression, accepting your lack of interest in picking up the pieces of your life. You feel you are not ready yet, but you also feel that you have been miserable for too long, and that your friends and family must think so too.

Only someone with a deep personal or professional

understanding of grieving can really appreciate how long recovery can take. I felt the awful frustration of having 'done all the right things': grieved; let my feelings 'hang out'; read the books; faced the facts; accepted . . . and *still* I was miserable! 'How long would this go on?' I screamed inside, and sometimes to my closest friends. For me, the intensity of despair lasted a full year, and for others it can be even longer. Unimaginable, I think, unless you have experienced it; so it isn't surprising if our friends and family become impatient.

I did consult a counsellor after Jack's death – some time later, when I seemed to be coping less and less well with my feelings. Immediately after the death your circle of family and friends pull together to support you, a vital crisis support system. But as time passes, others go back to their lives, and leave you to pick up the pieces of yours.

Except that I seemed incapable of doing that. I was desperately unhappy and infected my teenage children, who were otherwise ready to get on with living. They worried about me, hesitated to leave me alone, felt confused about their responsibility for me and helpless to lighten my misery. I, in turn, put pressure on them to be perfect; my only source of worth now was the excellence of my children. Impossible expectations at any time, but they themselves were feeling extremely anxious and insecure; they had been dealt a sharp lesson in the impermanence of life that they were busy trying to ignore.

So we scratched and sniped at each other, and were all becoming more and more miserable when grief counselling was suggested. We needed only a few sessions in various combinations – each of us separately, in pairs and all together. We uncovered the children's anxieties about my health (I was successfully treated for breast cancer the previous year); their anger at feeling they were not adequately informed about Jack's condition and the possibility of his death; my frustration with myself for not being a perfect mother. ('I have to be perfect', I protested to the counsellor, 'I'm all they've got'.)

We all reached a greater understanding of how depressed we were; how normal and natural this was; how difficult it was therefore to perform our everyday tasks; and how unrealistic were our expectations that we could do more than function at a fairly basic level for some time to come. We learned to share our feelings more, to show our love and concern, and to tolerate our 'failures' more sympathetically. I continued to hide my deepest despair from them, as I felt and still feel that young people should not have to shoulder the whole burden of a parent's grief. All the responsibilities of their own development, together with their own grief, are enough for them to deal with.

Perhaps my most valuable gain from this counselling was to understand that my grief was natural, acceptable and might take a long time to work through. I also accepted my reduced efficiency and competency – hard for me, as I have always prided myself on being able to cope with anything.

If you have been a happy, well-adjusted person who has led an enjoyable and fulfilling life, you will find your continuing depression and indifference to the world around you all the more frustrating. So it is easy to understand why many people experiencing the trauma of loss try to reject the feelings and seek relief in risk-taking. Teenagers drive fast, with or without a licence, shoplift, drink excessively (and so, for that matter, do adults). My teenage son dislocated his knee 10 days after Jack died; a friend's teenager was hit by a car two weeks after his mother's death. Both were accidents: we are less focused and careful when we are in shock. However, accidents are also made more likely by a need to deny our mortality, a bravado seen as the appropriate way to deal with trauma.

It is important for people suffering loss to be encouraged to recognise and accept their feelings. Some of us can do this on our own, although we may not necessarily recognise in ourselves the emotions and responses we observe and understand in others. Grief counselling is now widely accepted as an invaluable source of support, although the counsellor has no magic wand to take away your hurt. A list of counselling services is supplied in Appendix A.

Anticipating Death

If a partner's death is expected, the grieving begins as soon as you both understand that the illness is terminal.

When a terminal illness is diagnosed, we experience much of the sense of shock and disbelief that accompanies a sudden death. At first our conscious brain may reject absolutely the idea that our partner will die. We seek every conceivable treatment and cure, from the newest hi-tech clinical techniques to meditation and natural food remedies, even to faith-healers and apricot kernels, in our unwillingness to accept this medical 'death sentence'.

Yet at the same time our subconscious begins to process the revelation: we stop planning for the future and concentrate our thoughts and energies on the days and weeks immediately ahead. Our partner's welfare becomes our primary concern, and our lives are rearranged around hospital appointments, treatments at home, diet, notifying friends and family, mediating between the partner and those he or she does (or doesn't) want to see.

If your partner is in hospital, daily visits must somehow be managed, if not by you then by a roster of family and friends. Time must be found to talk to doctors who are never around when you are. And 'quality time' to spend with your children and others in your family, who are confused and anxious, and need the reassurance you may not feel able to give. Often we cannot find out what is likely to happen. Sometimes doctors are unavailable, or reluctant to consult with us; often they do not themselves know the answers to our worried questions of 'when?' and 'how?'.

Through all of this, our acceptance of loss begins to occur. Already our partner is no longer an equal, sharing the decisions and organisation of our life. He or she becomes the object of our concern, and although they will worry about you, and may notice that you are getting overtired or haven't the time to eat properly, it is outside their power to help you. Soon it's better for them to accept your care, and hope that others are giving you the support they can no longer provide.

This in itself is a cause for grieving: your partner may well mourn the loss of independence and equality in the relationship; you are losing your partner's practical assistance and support.

You can, however, continue to support each other emotionally, often long after physical independence is lost. If you can together recognise what is happening, it is possible to accept the changes and maintain a loving and mutually supporting relationship. You may want to seek help in working through these changes; hospitals have psychiatrists, psychologists and counsellors skilled in facilitating this process.

When Rex was dying, I was hurt that he seemed to lose interest in the day-to-day exploits of our small children. When the psychiatrist explained that he found the prospect of leaving them so painful that he needed to withdraw from their lives, I could understand his withdrawal, and cope with it.

Rex and I spent long hours together in the months before his death, holding each other, crying, talking a little, mostly about trivial things. We tried to reminisce about the wonderful times we had enjoyed together, but found it too painful. We touched on our children's future, but there wasn't a lot to say – we had discussed our hopes and fears for them since long before they were born, and had shared the same aspirations when they were growing up. He tried to reassure me that I would cope without him, and even fall in love and marry again, and be happy – but I didn't want to hear any of that. Later I did find it reassuring that those were his wishes for me, but at the time it seemed hard to believe and wholly irrelevant.

The more of your grief you can work through with your partner, the less you will be left to deal with on your own. Of course this is not always possible, and when it is, it varies enormously according to the circumstances of the illness, the nature of your relationship, and the ability of each partner to identify and talk about profound emotions.

Friends and family can help here too. You need to share the enormous burden of responsibility and your pain – with friends, family, a counsellor, often whoever happens to be there when the load feels too great to bear. But sometimes you don't want to talk about it; you want to be distracted, reminded that there is still life outside the hospital room and your own heavy heart. Get a friend to take you to a funny film, hire a comedy video, sit in the sun with your favourite music blasting in your ears. The day after Rex died, we all went to *The Muppet Movie*, and laughed ourselves silly. Truly, laughter *is* good medicine! (See Appendix B.)

Caring

Caring for a dying person demands all the resources you can muster. However deeply you love someone, it is hard always to have to put their needs first, especially when you are also suffering hurt and feel in need of care. Sometimes their demands may cause you to feel resentful – and then guilty about your resentment. Others are not always as understanding as you would hope them to be, and add to your burden by making you feel inadequate in other areas of your life.

When Rex was ill I had a difficult relationship with my supervisor at work. She took advantage of my vulnerability and pressured me to resign. I had to apply for leave for every moment's absence, as for example when I had to take Rex to hospital for treatment.

Others may not understand the enormity of your responsibility and the number of your chores. Some friends will be very sympathetic to your partner, but not notice all the ways in which your own life is being torn apart. This may cause you to resent them, or even your partner; hopefully you can share these feelings with your partner, rather than feel bitter or hurt. If you don't feel your partner can cope with this, find a friend who can, and at least share it with someone.

Relief

When a terminally ill partner finally dies, your first reaction is likely to be relief. You have suffered pain and anguish together: now it is over for your loved one, and you can stop worrying about him or her. Later you may feel guilty about it. Other people have expectations of suitable behaviour for the bereaved; and it is difficult not to feel that your behaviour is therefore inappropriate.

However odd it may seem – and may feel – this relief is perfectly natural and probably inevitable. Your life is no longer at your partner's disposal. This commonly elicits one of two responses: some feel that a great weight has been lifted from their shoulders; others feel that their reason for living has died, and that they might as well die too.

Relief, which I felt, will probably be temporary. I lived for a few weeks with a sense of unreality, unable to believe that the long-dreaded death had actually occurred. Then quite suddenly, when I felt physically rested and prepared to resume the burden of care, it struck me with great force that Rex was never coming back. This was not a temporary respite, but the end, the permanent loss of the man I loved, the partner in my life.

Guilt

You may continue to feel a combination of sadness and loss, relief and guilt. Some situations are undeniably easier, less stressful, less difficult now. You have been tied to the needs of another person, and you have denied or ignored many of your own. Now you can go to the pub with your mates, stay late at work to get something finished, play your music as loudly as you like. Yet it is the death of your partner that has made this possible, and enjoying your new freedoms may make you uneasy.

You must accept the reality that you can again enjoy some things which your partner's illness and your role as carer made impossible. You may feel disloyal to your partner at first, but it is a false feeling. You rejoice in loud music – but this does not signify that you are glad that your partner has died. Indulge yourself in this small pleasure, and in any others that appeal to you (see the list in Appendix B). The road back to a full and happy life is paved with these acceptances and pleasures.

As you heal, you may also feel guilt about not feeling miserable all the time. You may worry that accepting your partner's death means that you are forgetting them, that they were not as significant in your life as you thought they were. This is not so: if you loved and cared for your partner in life, you can accept and adjust more easily to their loss. Many people who have lost a loved partner develop a new relationship quite soon after the death.

If you are still carrying anger or resentment towards your partner, you may need to resolve those feelings before you can begin to let go and accept your partner's death. For this you may well need professional help; anger and resentment towards your partner are difficult emotions in life, and much more difficult in death.

Acceptance

Others who have cared for their partners through illness talk about the difficulty of believing the loss. They feel, deep down, that their partner has gone away for a short break from which they will surely return. Especially if we have lived with the knowledge of impending death, and yet our partner has still been there and able to share with us, it is more difficult to accept the reality of death when it finally comes.

Anger

Very few relationships make both partners perfectly happy. There is often tension, and indeed most partners sometimes wish to be without the other. If you happen to be in this stage of your relationship when your partner dies, you will experience widely mixed feelings: relief that they are gone, sadness that you will never be able to resolve the conflicts, and guilt that you were not caring enough or perhaps even wished them dead. You may also feel anger that in dying they have revived loving feelings you thought were gone, which now have no focus. Perhaps you no longer had any feeling left for your partner, and though you are relieved that they have died, you feel embarrassed that others expect you to be grieving. Again, the way we think people expect us to feel and to behave (and all too often they do!) can make us very uncomfortable.

Anger may be a large part of your feelings. Perhaps your partner had a weak heart, but refused to give up smoking or driving themselves too hard. Perhaps they were killed in an accident which was partly caused by their carelessness. It is natural when you are hurting to look for someone to blame. If it is your partner, you may feel a confusing mixture of anger, guilt and resentment, combined with sadness and loss.

In some relationships one partner is heavily dependent on the other. It may be financial dependence, if one is the sole earner. It may be social or emotional, where one partner keeps up with friends, or maintains contact with adult children, or expresses emotional support in time of crisis. You may well become angry with the partner who has left you to fend for yourself, and with yourself for having allowed your dependency to develop to such an extent. Try not to blame yourself or your partner, as this will not help you to resolve your feelings. If your anger persists for any length of time, talk it over with a counsellor.

Friends of mine had separated, and were beginning to make new lives for themselves when his cancer was diagnosed. His wife returned to nurse him, as there was still enough love and concern in their relationship for her to want to do this. But the situation puts a huge extra strain on both partners: it is hard for the sick person to be so dependent on an estranged partner, and difficult for the carer not to feel trapped and resentful.

When you know your partner is dying, you want to bring your life together to a satisfactory conclusion. This may include talking through issues that have concerned you, and resolving any long-standing conflict. But dying rarely changes a personality: if your partner has never openly demonstrated affection (buying you flowers, telling you they love you) it is unlikely that they will start now. It is not helpful, and it may even be destructive, to seek your partner's perfection in the short time remaining. It is a sufficient challenge to accept and love each other for what you are.

Some day, when you have worked through much of your grief, you will realise that you feel lighter and less unhappy. This is the beginning of your return to a full and happy life, and you should celebrate it. But be prepared to feel despondent again, for recovery is a bumpy ride, and you will experience many highs and lows before you complete your grieving.

3

Friends and Family

Many of us have not yet experienced the death of someone close. If this is the first death in your circle, many
of your family and friends will be at a loss to know how
to behave and how best to support you. You may find
that you need to help and guide your friends and family,
as they flounder in their efforts to help you. As with any
other traumatic experience, as we learn we grow.

Encourage your friends to read this book, or at least
this chapter, written especially for them. Feel free to
photocopy this section and hand it around, if you think
it might be helpful.

To the Friends:

There are as many possible responses to a friend's grief
as there are people – each of us is different, and each
will find different ways of expressing our concern, of
showing our love and offering our help. But I would
urge one thing upon you – DO respond! Those of us
who have not had an experience of death close to us, and
even some of us who have, will find it awkward to
broach the subject. We do not know what to say, and
we feel anxious lest we re-open a wound that may have
begun to heal. Many well-meaning friends therefore say
nothing, perhaps believing that it is best to 'carry on',
to behave as if nothing has happened, to try to be as
normal as possible. This can be terribly hurtful, and give

your grieving friend the feeling that fear of embarrassment is your main concern.

Your friend's life is no longer as it was. An earthquake has ripped life apart, and a hole now gapes where once there was a warm and loving partnership. If you avert your eyes, if you pretend not to see the hole, you deny the most significant event in your friend's life. If you do this, you may hurt your friend: you will also reduce all conversation to trivial and increasingly meaningless chit-chat.

Of course there will be more and less appropriate times to signal your concern. Control is important for the bereaved at this time, and the death of a loved one is the greatest loss of control one may ever experience. There is no way back, no possible mediation, no hope, no future. Suddenly, every happy memory simply reminds you of what is lost. Daily routines become meaningless. Worse than all this, everything you dreamed together, all the things you ever talked about or shared as hopes for the future, are gone – completely. You seem to lose the capacity to direct your life. Past, present and future have lost their purpose, and you lack the ability and the will to make decisions or to set goals. Grief and sadness keep overwhelming you, tears flow when you don't want them to, your mind is a fog and your capacity to focus on anything other than your loss seems to have disappeared.

The area of your friend's life in which they can most easily regain some control is often work. Almost everyone has a part of their life, whether in a paid job, in the garden, or somewhere in the community, where they are accustomed to working independently of their partner. If the partner was not previously there every day, it will soon become possible to engage in some activities where their absence is not constantly obvious. Here, at least, your friend can hope for some control, and for many people this is necessary in order to keep going.

A teacher friend, grieving for a lost baby, was frustrated and distressed when, on her way to class and feeling in control, a colleague expressed her sympathy – and unwittingly undid that carefully contrived control. I, on the other hand, welcomed and even looked for expressions of concern from friends and colleagues, and wept freely for weeks, at work and at home. Yet I too experienced the frustration of not being able to finish a sentence, of trying unsuccessfully to stave off the tears until I had managed to put into words an emotion I wanted to express. And I raged at always feeling down, at never feeling light-hearted, content or free of pain.

It may seem difficult, but it IS always better to say something than to remain silent. It is even better, however, to choose the right time to speak. Since everyone has different needs, it is very important to try to understand how your friend is coping, so that you can choose the best time to speak. If you have any choice, it is probably best to avoid times when your friend appears to be in control of a work situation.

What Do You Say?

It is not necessary to say very much; indeed there is very little one can legitimately say. What you can do is register your own shock, disbelief and sense of loss. In doing this you mirror your friend's feelings. In sharing your feelings, you show that theirs are natural and appropriate. You may also comfort your friend, who may now recognise that you have some understanding of their loss.

It may not at first be appropriate to say any more than this, but soon it will be very important to reminisce with your friend about their partner. A grieving person wants very much to share memories with others for whom the partner was also important; to have a sense that the partner was a person of significance, not only for themselves, but also for others. So be ready to talk about the partner, to remind your friend of good times you all shared, of funny or insightful things the partner said to you, of a kindness by which you will always remember him or her.

Do:

- say how sorry you are.
- mention the person's name.
- choose your time.
- share your memories as soon as you feel your friend is ready to do so.

Don't:

- say 'I know how you feel'. No one knows how another person feels; the bereaved's emotions are theirs alone.
- say 'It will soon feel better'. This may be true, but your friend must discover this alone, and in time. Right now, it simply trivialises their loss.
- compare the loss with anyone else's. This is irrelevant to your friend, and hurtful.
- suggest that it could have been worse. Nothing could feel worse to your friend at this time, and to suggest it is meaningless and wounding.
- say 'I suppose it was for the best', or suggest that it is a relief. This does not correspond to the way your friend is feeling.

What Can You Do?

As soon as the death occurs family and friends need to be informed. Yet this is one of the hardest things for the bereaved person to do. When Pamela's husband rang me with the news of her death, I offered to ring some of our mutual friends, and was able to help him ensure that they were all informed. As most of us have several different groups of friends and colleagues, a friend from each group offering this help can be immensely useful and reassuring. In the shock after a death, it is an extra concern that you may forget to notify someone who would really want to know.

Small acts of practical assistance are most appropriate. For example, when you visit, take a cake, or some soup, or a casserole. Or offer to cut some wood, mow the lawn, wash the dishes. But be tactful and sensitive to your friend's feelings. If your offer of help implies that your friend has lost control of the practicalities of life, you may give more hurt than healing.

A little while after Jack died, my mother (who lived next door) tried to take over my washing for me. I understood why she wanted to do this: she is a warm, practical person, who was hurting so much with my pain and the injustice of our loss that she needed to *do* something to help me. She and my stepfather gave me so much assistance and support in so many ways, all of which I welcomed and was grateful for. But the washing was too much – I felt I would be giving up control over an important part of my responsibility, admitting that I couldn't cope. Refusing her offer was difficult and painful for both of us; but her love and respect for me were great enough to allow her to accept my decision.

There are no clear-cut solutions: each family will need to work out their own ways of helping and supporting each other.

To the Bereaved:

Let others help you. In offering assistance they meet their needs, whether to assuage their grief, or apply their balm to yours, or both. You need not feel obliged to them; in meeting their own needs, they do not obligate you. The more you can guide your friends and family to understand your feelings and to meet your needs, the more strength and love you will all gain from each other.

4

Immediately

Understanding the Event

When someone you love actually dies, it is not possible to grasp the full meaning of the event at once. If you have thought about your partner's death, you will feel some of the impact: you may be aware that he or she will never again hold you or lie beside you; you may feel anxious about how to tell family and friends; you may anticipate some of the yawning emptiness that lies ahead.

But the full meaning of your partner's death takes quite a long time to make itself felt. You feel numb for a while; your mind cannot encompass all the ways in which you have needed, depended on, accepted and enjoyed your partner's support.

For weeks, months even, you continue to be surprised by situations in which you miss your partner's presence. Many annual events – birthdays, Christmas, anniversaries, the change of seasons – drive home your loss, especially the first time you experience them without your partner.

The emotions you experience during this time are what people mean by grief. You have to bear them, go with them, share them when you can, work through them, until – difficult as this now seems to you – they begin to hurt less.

I remember sitting at the kitchen bench, sobbing, my heart breaking. I had come out to breakfast before the others, and sat on a stool. Suddenly I knew that Jack would never again come up behind me and put his arm around me, the way he did so often in the early morning. I felt my life was over. But day by day it became easier; and so we put our lives together again, slowly and painfully, but nevertheless we do.

These adjustments occur slowly, and we must give them time, but there are things we need to do immediately.

Saying Goodbye

When a loved one dies, you need time to say goodbye if this is at all possible. We grow up believing that death is frightening, and that the body after death is strange and alien. But this is simply the body of your beloved partner, from which the life has gone. Unless it was a violent death, the body is just as it was when your partner was alive, and it is not at all frightening to sit with one you have loved, hold their hand, kiss their face, smooth their hair, hug their body.

When Rex died, he had been in pain for some time, and I had touched him gingerly, for fear of hurting him. When he died, and was no longer in pain, I lay beside him and hugged him tightly, releasing some of my pent-up anguish in this urgent physical act.

After Jack died, I sat beside him and held his hand, stroked his hair, talked to him as if he could still hear me; and so, later on, did his children.

I was very fortunate to be able to farewell both my men in this way, having time to begin to come to terms with the awful reality. Many family and friends have attested to the importance of having time to spend with the one who has died; my niece writes of how 'comforting and calming' it was to keep her father, then a year later her mother, at home for several hours after each died.

Hospitals and doctors generally accept the need for this time-honoured custom, and adjust hospital schedules to accommodate it. Even in the intensive care unit where Jack died, there was no pressure on us to hurry, and it was several hours before all the family members were satisfied that they had properly said goodbye.

Registering the Death

A death should be registered within five days of the event, in the sub-district where it occurred. A doctor completes a medical certificate of cause of death, which must be taken by an informant (often the partner, usually a relative) to the office of the Registrar of Births, Deaths and Marriages. These offices are listed in the Yellow Pages; and your local registrar will give you information about other offices if you need it.

The informant gives the details which are entered in the register; a copy of this entry is the death certificate. The Registrar's office also issues a certificate of registration of death, which is specifically for the Department of Social Security. This confirms that the death has been registered, and has questions on the back which enable a partner to begin to identify benefits and make appropriate claims.

The certificate of registration of death is free; copies of the death certificate cost £2.50 each. If you think you will need several copies you should buy them; some organisations (such as insurance companies) will accept a photocopy of the death certificate certified by a solicitor or Justice of the Peace (listed in the Yellow Pages). You may need to ask people what documentation they require. You can buy further copies of the death certificate later if you find you need them.

Letting People Know

As soon as practicable, family, friends and acquaintances need to be informed. I wanted this to be done quickly, to avoid the embarrassment of having to deal with people who were unaware of the death. Yet it is almost impossible to make all these calls yourself. The news is simply too heavy to keep repeating. You could perhaps tell people face to face, but it is difficult to tell them by phone, when you cannot see or touch each other. Phoning is something that family and friends might be happy to do for you (see 'Friends and Family'). There are a few people you may feel you need to tell yourself; but everyone will understand if they receive the news from someone else, and will be grateful that you have thought to have them told.

You can quickly make a list of family and friends. I added all the people I was likely to encounter in the next few weeks – neighbours, chemist, newsagent, any shopkeepers you deal with regularly. If your partner died in hospital or away from home, make sure your local GP is told – hospitals are sometimes slow in passing on patient information. Don't rely too much on the grapevine; it usually has gaps, and it is awkward to discover weeks later that someone who knew your partner quite well is still not aware of their death.

Even more difficult than face-to-face encounters are the telephone callers who ask for your partner. Children find this particularly distressing; mine just handed me the phone, or asked the caller to ring back later and speak to me. Although you avoid as much of this as you can, it does inevitably happen, and you may need to talk to other family members about what to say.

A particular problem may arise if your partner ran a business from home. We recently chose a plumber from the Yellow Pages. We phoned, and had to be told by the poor widow that her husband had recently died. If you can afford it, an answerphone on which you (or a friend) record a message may be better than having to repeat this sad message frequently yourself.

Department of Social Security

If you are dependent on Social Security benefits, or have been left with no money, you should contact the Department as soon as you can, so that your new situation can be sorted out and your claim for benefit processed quickly.

A widow's payment of £1000 can be made very quickly if needed – this is intended to cover immediate needs such as urgent living costs and funeral expenses. Most wives will be eligible for this payment, and the Department can establish eligibility very easily. Take your marriage certificate with you if you have not previously shown it to the DSS. Unfortunately there is no equivalent payment for de facto partners, widowers or gay or lesbian partners.

You may also be eligible for the widowed mother's allowance if you have young children, or the widow's pension if you are older. Take or send the certificate of registration of the death which is intended for the DSS. If your partner was receiving benefits you will need to return his or her pension and allowance books (but keep a note of the pension or allowance number). Ask for assistance and a DSS officer will explain your entitlements and help you with the forms.

Financial Matters

Your situation will depend on the kind of bank account/s you have. Funds in joint accounts where the signatories are 'tenants in common' (the normal arrangement in the

United Kingdom) automatically become the property of the survivor, whether or not you are married. This money is not part of your partner's estate. If the account needs only one signature, you can continue to operate it as usual. If it needs two signatures, or if the account is set up differently, you will have to check with the bank. Take the death certificate and, if you have it, a copy of the will so that they can establish what you are entitled to.

If the account is in your partner's name, it is part of the estate. You will need to discuss this with your bank manager: if your partner left the bulk of the estate to you, you will need to show the bank a copy of the will as well as the death certificate. They may then release some money to you, continue to make mortgage payments and so on, but you will need to discuss that with the bank.

Fourteen years ago, when a spouse's right to continue to use a joint bank account was less certain, I withdrew the little money we had from our joint account as soon as Rex was no longer able to operate it.

Hopefully you will have at least some understanding of your partner's (or your joint) financial arrangements – you may have been responsible for the bills and the budget. If not, you will need help from a friend, a family member, a solicitor or an accountant. The man who helped me with Jack's tax forms became a friend and financial advisor, as well as an occasional shoulder to cry on.

Not all business firms are perfectly efficient, so it is quite likely that you will receive bills which have already been paid. There are also a few firms which invent bills to send to bereaved households, assuming that everyone will be too distressed to challenge them. Make sure you keep all receipts, and check all incoming bills against them. Phone the company if you doubt a particular bill, and do not pay it until you are satisfied that it is genuine. A friend can help you to organise the paperwork, but you need to take control as soon as possible.

You will need copies of the death certificate and the will in a number of situations: the bank will be happier for you to make any adjustment to your account when they have seen the death certificate and (if you have it) a will leaving the bulk of the estate to you; some organisations such as pension and superannuation funds and insurance companies ask to see a copy of the death certificate when being notified of the death.

The Funeral

Next, you must think about the funeral. This is the public (or private) event which formally marks the end of your partner's life. It is discussed fully in 'The Funeral'. Try to make the ceremony as your partner would have wanted it, but also include as much as possible of what will comfort you, as it can be a valuable release of emotion for you and your family.

Legal Matters

Make an appointment to see a solicitor to discuss the will, clarify your financial position, and begin the procedure of having probate granted. (This is the legal process of accepting the provisions of the will; money cannot be disbursed, title deeds changed etc. until this is done. If the will is straightforward it may only take a few weeks; otherwise it can be months or even years.) If there was no will, or you cannot find it, you need to see a solicitor as soon as possible.

If you don't have a solicitor, a friend or family member may recommend one. If not, contact your local Citizens'

Advice Bureau – there are offices in all large towns. They can provide a list of solicitors to choose from.

Other Assistance

Social workers in the Social Services Department of your local Borough or County Council can help you with many practical problems. You can contact them at your local Town or County Hall.

Checklist of Things To Do

Here is a checklist of things to be done after your partner's death:

- make sure the death is notified to the Registrar of Births, Deaths and Marriages;

- notify family, friends, work, local doctor, etc;

- establish your financial position – make sure you have access to enough money to live on for a couple of months;

- if you are living in rented accommodation, check with your local Citizens' Advice Bureau about your rights;

- contact the Department of Social Security;

- notify the bank, post office, building society or any other institution where your partner had an account;

- discuss funeral arrangements with close family or friends – clearly establish your own wishes, together with any that your partner expressed;

- decide whether or not you want cards printed – announcing your partner's death and/or acknowledging flowers and messages of condolence; organise this if you do (examples in Appendix C);

- notify meals-on-wheels or home help that these are no longer needed;

- locate the will and make an appointment with a solicitor;

- get copies of the death certificate and the will, certified by a solicitor or JP if necessary;

- draft a 'form letter' (see 'Mail' and Appendix D) to send to businesses, department stores, mailing lists, gas, electricity, telephone etc;

- keep all bills and receipts and check all incoming bills against those already paid;

- find one or more recent photos of your partner, for yourself, and have copies made for friends who would like one. Often this is what they ask for as a memento;

- contact any insurance companies or Friendly Societies your partner may have had policies with. These include:
  - life insurance (in order to claim)
  - car/house/contents insurance (in order to change to your name or the name of the estate until probate is granted);

- return library books or records to avoid reminders and fines;

- return your partner's driving licence with the date of death (and request a refund for the unused portion);

- notify the tax inspector;

- think about sharing some of your partner's possessions with close family and friends (see 'Possessions').

5

The Funeral

Rex

Before I came to terms with Rex's approaching death, I had a fear, almost a contempt, of funerals. Rex and I used to joke with our friends about not having a funeral. Instead we talked of having a wake where everyone was hearty and jolly, and told funny stories about the one who had died. Indeed, Rex had written something like this into his will.

Now naive we were! How untouched by the real tragedy of the death and loss of loved ones! As Rex's death came nearer, I began to worry about our thoughtlessness and to feel that I would want – would need – an event to mark the end of his life in a public, formal, respectful way. This, then, is a funeral: not necessarily full of religious assertions (which would have been foreign to us, but might be just what a committed believer wants), but nonetheless a ceremony. What was needed was a rite of passage, when all our friends and colleagues would gather to mark his passing.

He agreed readily to my change of heart. There are few occasions in life when everyone important to you comes together to pay tribute; I think he was grateful that we who loved him needed to honour him one last time in this way.

When he finally accepted his approaching death, he wrote a list of people to be notified of the funeral, and titled it – his wry irreverence with him to the end – 'The Last Round-up'.

The funeral director took care of most of the practical details, though there are a number of decisions to be made (see later in this chapter). It is possible to pre-arrange and pre-pay a funeral, which we had done, and which enables the dying person to participate in making the decisions if they want to (see Appendix E).

So we concentrated on the music, as I wanted to farewell him to the sounds he had taught me to love as dearly as he did. A friend and I spent hours listening to his old records and choosing jazz and blues for the occasion.

The day of the funeral was cool and drizzly. I felt it was fitting: the heavens were weeping too for this fine, much loved man. All our friends and family were there, and I was immensely comforted when they hugged me, expressing their love and compassion for both of us. An expected death lacks the shock and disbelief of a sudden one, yet there is still incomprehension, terrible sadness and a sense of injustice that a life has been cut short with so much still to give.

Our recorded music ushered us into the chapel. Two old and dear friends spoke about Rex's – our – life while I wept freely. Another friend taped the service, as I wanted a record of it. I also wanted it for the children, who were not present. I judged that they had had enough: they had seen their father fade to a shadow, felt him loosen his emotional bonds with them as he prepared to leave them, traipsed endlessly back and forth to the hospital, lived in the shadow of grief for too long already. I also felt unable to meet their needs in addition to my own, and readily accepted that they did not want to attend. I now believe it would have been better for them to go to the funeral, and to participate with the rest of the family in this final farewell. There are, of course, particular needs of children which must be met, and I discuss these more fully later in this chapter.

Jack

Jack's death, on the other hand, struck unexpectedly. There were more people to consider: he had grown-up children and parents still living. But I held fast to two notions: for all their terrible sadness and loss, mine was greater; and I knew Jack best. So I guided the event which was the funeral, feeling that it was the last thing I could do for him, and it must be done as well as possible. We had a few days before the funeral, as I wanted enough time to let people know. I knew, better than Jack ever did, how much love and respect he inspired in so many friends and colleagues.

In the notice for the paper we mentioned all the closest family, including his children, my children, a friend who was like a son to him, his parents and sister, and his ex-wife. Thank Heavens times have changed since some newspapers would only accept the names of legally married spouses and their children in their notices! How much hurt that heartless rule must have inflicted on grieving families and friends.

For music I chose the Mozart requiem which Jack and I had discovered together. The chapel at the crematorium was filled to overflowing. All the children and I sat in the front row, and as the service began I looked around at all his friends and colleagues who had come to say goodbye and to share our grieving. Through my tears I whispered to the others 'Look at all the people who loved Jack'. Three friends spoke movingly about his life, as family and friends wept together. Exhausting though it was, I found it immensely comforting to share this experience with so many friends, and to feel their expressions of sorrow.

Jean

A year later, Jack's former mother-in-law died. I was very apprehensive about going to the funeral, as it was in the same chapel as Jack's had been, and that experience still felt very raw. Yet I wanted to extend to others in the family the same support and comfort they had given me. The service was a more traditional funeral, with a minister speaking about Jean's life, and how she had passed into the next and happier life, finally free of sorrow and pain, where she would await her family joyfully. I found it less personal and less direct, but others were comforted and consoled by the familiar beauty of the words and music and the sense of continuity the traditional funeral service brings. Here you know that generations have died and been farewelled with the same words and music, and this will go on for generations to come. The understanding that countless unknown others have shared the same ritual, that you are therefore not on your own, but part of the millennia of human life, is one of the great strengths of these traditions.

Pamela

Pamela's funeral was different again. She had thought about the ceremony, chosen the church, talked with the minister and the friend who read the lesson. Another close friend gave a deeply moving eulogy, and the prayers were a mixture of traditional and non-traditional. They included the Lord's Prayer and Psalm 23, and also this adaptation of the Sermon on the Mount:

> There is no difficulty that enough love will not
>   conquer;
> no disease that enough love will not heal;

no door that enough love will not open;
no gulf that enough love will not bridge;
no wall that enough love will not throw down;
no sin that enough love will not redeem . . .

It makes no difference how deeply seated may be the trouble; how hopeless the outlook; how muddled the tangle; how great the mistake. A sufficient realisation of love will dissolve it all. If only you could love enough you would be the happiest and most powerful being in the world.

I was honoured to help carry Pamela's coffin into the crematorium chapel. Taking my hand away from the coffin handle was the final act of letting her go, and it was almost more than any of us could bring ourselves to do.

Although she was no longer a practising Christian, she and her husband felt that since they were both raised in the Christian tradition, the service would give comfort and healing which reached back into childhood. Her husband wrote that 'it was all devastatingly wounding and at the same time – as Pamela anticipated – a statement of a kind of finality, and the first touch of healing'.

I think, too, the very ritual quality of a familiar service provides a secure framework for a harrowing emotional experience. The funeral is a mile post, the last formal farewell to the one you have loved and lost, which for many grieving partners is an appalling ordeal, something to be 'got through', often with great difficulty. The formal service will meet the needs of many bereaved people, numbed or incapacitated by their loss. It is likely that many will experience the funeral as if in a daze, and afterwards remember little, except perhaps an enormous sense of relief when it is over.

Children

It can be difficult for children to endure a funeral service, but it is equally important for them to take part in it, as their grief has to be channelled just as much as that of adults. I did not insist on my children coming to Rex's funeral, partly because I did not think I could cope with their grief as well as my own. This is a real problem, but it can be resolved by another adult taking responsibility for them: explaining the funeral service, acknowledging everyone's grief, allowing them to cry – or not to cry – and giving them a sense of safety. Their presence therefore recognises their importance as members of the family who participate together in saying goodbye.

Arranging the Funeral

You should have several days in which to plan the funeral service. There are a number of decisions to make. These include:

- when and where the service will be (you will have at least two days' grace, and the service may be as much as a week after the death);
- the choice of cremation or burial (where your cultural or religious background permits a choice);
- a funeral director;
- how much you want to spend;
- the wording of the death notice for the paper;
- who you want to speak about your partner;
- the music;
- whether you prefer friends to send flowers, or donations to the Heart Foundation, Cancer Research, etc;
- whether you want a book signed by those who attend, photos, etc;

- the reception afterwards.

The Yellow Pages list funeral directors, and you can get an idea from the size and wording of the advertisements of the general style and likely cost. I looked for those who described their services as 'simple' and 'inexpensive'. I rang a few and obtained detailed quotes, which should cover:

- notice/s in newspaper/s;
- flowers;
- coffin;
- booking crematorium/cemetery/church;
- someone to officiate at the service if you wish.

Although this is an intensely emotional event, it is also a business transaction. You should therefore get at least a couple of quotes from funeral directors, once you are reasonably clear about what you want. Too many people are persuaded by funeral directors to spend money unnecessarily, in the mistaken view that the amount of money spent on a funeral is a measure of your love and respect. Of course, if you can afford to, and feel that a service 'with everything', including the most expensive coffin with trimmings, is a necessary part of the ritual for you, this is fine. However, it is not necessary to spend a great deal of money to honour your partner; sharing your grief with family and friends in a simple service is the essential part of this ceremony.

It is important that the service reflects the person who has died, as far as this is possible. If the officiating clergy did not know your partner, try to get a friend or family member to speak also. A polished speech is not what you need; rather a heartfelt remembrance of the person you have all come together to farewell.

A cautionary note: it is not uncommon for houses to

be robbed while everyone is out attending the funeral service. Ask a friend to remain at home during the service, to avoid this shocking possibility.

Cremation

Cremation is usually arranged by a funeral director. Most of the service can take place in a church, followed by a procession to the crematorium; the words of committal are spoken in the crematorium itself. Otherwise the whole service can be held in the crematorium chapel. The time made available for a cremation is usually quite limited – 15 to 20 minutes as a rule. Within this period you can arrange the service as you wish, and choose whether or not to have a cleric to officiate.

Burial

Anyone whose permanent address is within an ecclesiastical parish is in theory entitled to be buried in the parish churchyard. In practice, there may be no space left in the churchyard. Some churches have burial grounds separated from the church, where parishioners have the right of burial. The vicar, rector or priest in charge and the parochial church council make decisions about who to accept, and what fees will apply. The costs of an organist or other musician/s, extra heating and the digging of the grave are additional.

Most cemeteries are non-denominational, and run either by a local authority or a privately owned company. In most cemeteries, any type of religious service (or none at all) can be held. Most cemeteries have a chapel which is non-denominational, and some provide a roster of clergy of different denominations. Fees vary widely; you should enquire as to what they are, what they cover, and what regulations apply. For example, some will not allow flowers to be planted or put on graves; others have restrictions on headstones or memorial monuments. Exclusive right to the grave may not exist at all, or may only apply for a fixed number of years. You should ask your funeral director if you don't wish to approach the cemetery directly.

The family may already own a burial plot (called a deed of grant or a certificate of ownership), or the right to use of a grave in a churchyard (called a faculty). You need to inform the funeral directors, who will make the necessary arrangements. If no burial plot is owned, or if you wish to have your partner buried in a cemetery that is more convenient for you, you can buy a burial plot yourself. The plot is bought from the cemetery, and you can choose a grave without the right to exclusive burial (the least expensive), a grave with the right of exclusive burial, or a lawn grave, where you can only put up a very simple headstone, leaving the rest of the grave grass.

Friends whose daughter died chose a plot on gently sloping ground near some magnificent gum trees – a beautiful, peaceful place. Their other children were attracted to the idea of a grave with a large commemorative headstone: but on seeing the untidiness and disrepair of the older gravestones, they readily opted for a grave in the modern, lawn-cemetery section, with its small plaque and rosebush.

Many of those who attend the service may choose not to join the funeral cortege to the cemetery. The graveside ceremony is brief – a few prayers if it is a religious funeral, as the coffin is lowered into place. For many who have been bereaved, there is a merciful kind of blankness at this moment, though others may feel a shocking sense that this is the final moment of parting.

Feelings about future visits to the grave vary widely. Some feel compelled to make such visits, finding at the graveside an opportunity for peaceful reflection, for making time in a busy life to pay sad tribute to a lost loved one. Others like to bring flowers regularly, keeping up a lifetime's habit of tending and caring. Still others prefer to remember experiences shared, or think of their partner as being in heaven, and rarely if ever visit the grave. In this, as in so many things, your own feelings dictate what is appropriate.

After the Funeral

Friends collected the flowers that were sent to the chapel, so that we could take them home. (Funeral directors will also do this for you if you ask them.) I wanted the flowers at home; I also needed the cards to acknowledge all the expressions of sympathy.

I asked my brother to take photos of those who came to the service. It was of course done discreetly, as it is unusual and may even seem inappropriate to some people. I did it because a funeral is such an emotionally overpowering occasion that it is difficult to take everything in, and yet later on I wanted to remember who came to say goodbye. (Directors will provide an attendance book to be signed by those who attend the service; this serves the same purpose. You may need to ask for this; it is becoming more common, but is by no means universal.)

We invited everyone home to share a drink and something to eat, and most of them came. I was anxious not to be left alone, and wanted to hold on to the warmth and solidarity generated by the service. The service itself can be an expression of solidarity, leaving everyone with a need to talk. They may need to extend their emotional support to you, and share with each other their sense of loss. The reception can be in your own home, if you wish, or at a friend's, if you feel you may prefer to be on your own quite soon, but don't want to break up the gathering too quickly. Funeral directors will also arrange this if you wish them to; of course you will have to pay for it.

Whichever you choose, you do not need to prepare the food yourself – you have quite enough to deal with on this day, and you need space to be overwhelmed by your emotions. If you cope better when you have something to do, offer to help, but it may be unwise to take on the responsibility yourself – you may find it becomes the last straw! If you can afford to, employ a caterer to provide sandwiches, glasses, drinks, cups of tea and coffee (or ask a friend to get the caterer); otherwise close friends and family are usually more than happy to do something practical. This is also a way for them to feel less helpless, and to relieve some of their own feelings of pain and loss.

After the funeral, when friends and family have finally gone home, when all the energy you channelled into surviving the service has achieved its purpose and been exhausted, and you may find yourself alone in a near-empty house, the sickening reality of your partner's absence – permanent, not temporary – finally begins to make itself felt.

What will you do now? How can life ever make any sense again? You *will* be able to live a full life again, but (perhaps) not for a while. In the meantime, as a friend wrote to me, you will need to 'go on putting one foot in front of the other, until it comes naturally again'.

The Ashes

Crematoria offer several options for dealing with the ashes. Scattering the ashes is a popular, rather romantic idea, but carrying out your partner's wishes can be painful, and it is worth discussing this beforehand if possible.

Rex wanted his ashes scattered, but with no particular

location specified, I was free to choose to have them scattered on the crematorium rose garden. This meant that I didn't have to be involved, for which I was grateful.

Jack had specified a particular spot for the scattering of his ashes, where he had been especially happy and free as a child. Since this was in the country and other members of his family needed to be consulted about the spot, it snowballed into a large family excursion, on a day which happened to be cold, wet and bleak, on a muddy, slippery hillside down to a river's edge.

I found this experience much more gruelling and stark than the funeral itself. Though it was months after Jack's death, it revived all the raw emotions of the earlier occasion, but more nakedly – no flowers or music, just the wind, the rain, the mud and the ashes of the man I loved – all that physically remained of him – in a grey plastic container too big to conceal in a pocket or handbag.

At the water's edge I read aloud the description of the spot from the paper he had written it on, said goodbye, and poured the ashes into the river, while the large group of twenty or so family and friends huddled under umbrellas and wept.

Although we then climbed back up the hill, and were soon home with family, warm, dry and companionable, I couldn't shake my feeling of despair; indeed it did not lift until well into the following day, when I was on my way back to the city and my still lonely, but more 'normal' life, in which I was again beginning to exercise some control.

With hindsight, I could have carried out Jack's wishes without quite so high an emotional cost if I had taken the ashes quietly and with only one or two others to guide me. I believe that this is a private, not a public event, and that you only have to take account of your own needs. You have a responsibility to your partner, but unlike the funeral, it is an occasion for private grieving, a very personal farewell.

6

Children

Young Children

My children sometimes drove me crazy. More often, and more important, they kept me sane. When Rex died, Michael was nine and Rachel seven. They knew their father was dying, although Michael, the more 'rational' of the two, couldn't quite believe that if he was in hospital, they couldn't make him better. Rachel understood, at some deeper emotional level, that her daddy was leaving her. After Rex's death, Mike was able to cry, talk about how he felt, and work some way through his grief within the family. However, at school he behaved as though nothing had happened, and whenever possible avoided admitting that he no longer had a father.

Rachel on the other hand, said little, but her behaviour deteriorated: she kicked out at me and clung to me by turns. It took me weeks, and much talking with good friends, to recognise her behaviour as an expression of anger at her father's death. As soon as I held her and said, 'I know you are behaving like this because you are angry that Daddy died. We are angry too, and sad, but please don't be angry with us' she began to recover. It didn't happen overnight, but my understanding of her anger was the beginning of her acceptance of her father's loss.

Specialists say it is important to help distressed children identify their own feelings. If you offer an explanation, the child will accept it if it fits, and discard it if not. So it can't hurt to try. You are also letting them know that you understand the relationship between their feelings and behaviour.

For me, their needs became paramount, and I tried to keep the household on an even keel for their sake. On my own, I felt I could have gone to bed and stayed there indefinitely. What did life hold after all? It felt as if all the good times had ended with Rex's death. But the children were there, and needed me. Naturally, I did not only respond to their needs, but sometimes also resented them. When they grieve, young children often regress, and make emotional demands which seem unreasonable and burdensome. Sometimes when they demanded my emotional support, I felt that I had nothing left to give.

If you have children, their demands may be oppressive, but the way ahead is clear. If you don't, you may need to focus on someone (or something – job, garden, voluntary work) that needs you, so you feel there is still a role for you after your partner's death.

Teenagers

When Jack died my children were older, and we were more able to grieve together. They helped to pick up the extra load which is created with one adult less in the household. Yet they were not adult, and they retained a child's capacity to deal with one day at a time. The endless lonely future did not loom for them as ominously as it did for me. So I shared my sadness and my tears with them, but not completely. If they were able to be happy sometimes, I would not spoil it for them. I encouraged them to go out and have fun, and tried to hide the awful depths of my misery. Bereavement does not alter the fact that teenagers need to live part of their lives outside the home: for them the experience is quite different from that of small children or adults.

Taking Your Partner's Place

There is a common expectation, when a parent dies, that the oldest child (in some households the oldest male child) should accept some of that parent's role. Other people often encourage this expectation unthinkingly, for example by saying to a small boy: 'You'll have to be the man of the house, won't you?', or to a girl, 'You'll have to look after Daddy now'.

Comforting as this role may be at the time, for both the child and the surviving parent, it can create problems for the future which might be better avoided from the beginning. To expect children to behave like adults makes it doubly hard for them to express their childish fears, anxiety and grief. My niece, who lost first her father and then her mother, expressed it as the loss, among many other things, of the place where 'you can always be a child, however old you are'. Since children often develop an irrational, but nevertheless deep, sense of guilt for a parent's death, it is important to encourage them to express their feelings in as open, natural and childlike a way as is possible.

It was months after Rex's death before Rachel let on that she felt it was her fault that Daddy died. Rex had cancer, first diagnosed from a sore back. Rachel loved to be carried, long after she ceased to be a lightweight. So, in her child's mind, she had given Daddy his sore back and then he had died. This kind of revelation comes much more readily from a child who is allowed to be childlike than from one who has adopted the stoical, 'grown-up' behaviour felt to be expected of them. Obviously you need to know your children's thoughts and feelings, so that you can deal with them sympathetically and rationally.

A New Relationship

Another problem arises if you begin to develop a new relationship. The more your child has 'become' your partner, bringing you an early morning cuppa, sharing your decisions about the household or the younger children, enjoying the confidences of a partner, the more difficult it will be for them to 'move over' and let someone else into the family circle.

Michael had this problem when Jack and I began living together. He was jealous of this new man in my life, and resentful that I seemed to have forgotten his dad so easily. I was feeling guilty too: on the one hand, six months is not long to complete your grieving; on the other, it is an eternity of loneliness and of longing to be loved again.

Children's jealousy, and your own awkwardness, often focus on the intimacy of a new relationship. This is especially so as you begin a relationship, which is when you are more likely to be physically demonstrative. Your children may contrast this with the different stage you were at with your partner. Younger children feel excluded when you no longer want them in bed with you. Many bereaved partners are content to have their children in bed with them after their partner has died. It provides comfort when you and they have trouble sleeping (see also 'Fatigue'). The longer it continues, however, after the most urgent need has passed, the more excluded they will feel when someone else tries to take 'their' place in your bed.

The relationship between your children and your new partner is likely to be difficult. Much as you want to be loved and for all of you to become a family as smoothly as possible, you do not want to blot out your previous partner. The children need to keep their parent's memory alive, and will need your active assistance in this. Immediately after a death, it takes an effort to recall someone who has died, and to include them naturally in your conversation. Grandparents often find this particularly difficult, as in their generation people may be more reluctant to speak – well or ill – of the dead.

I had to force myself at first to bring Rex's name into everyday conversations, as the loss was still painful, and I was reluctant to upset people. It is important, however. 'Remember when Daddy took you to see that film?' reinforces a happy memory, and also gives your children permission to talk about the parent when they want to.

Your new partner is also likely to have difficulty adjusting to their new family. If they have agreed to share the parenting with you, they will have expectations about their rights and their role. Some new step-parents want to embrace the children as their own; younger children may slip easily into this role. Yet both desires create problems, since they deny a place for the children's real parent, and make it more difficult for them to keep a healthy and happy memory alive.

Even older children can feel intense jealousy towards a new partner. It is your right to go on developing your own relationships, and you may want to build an intimate one. It is also your children's right to go on needing you, and needing your help, love and understanding to adjust to the new developments in your life.

I hope you do fall in love again, and have the chance to experience these difficulties.

You May Need Professional Help

Children experience a wide range of emotions on a parent's death, and perhaps especially that of a step-parent. They grieve certainly, but perhaps the death also resolves their jealousy of your partner, and now they can have you to themselves. Or if there was some tension between you and your partner, or between the children and you or your partner, this may now be relieved. But their relief will be tinged by guilt when you are clearly so bereft.

Many of these complicated feelings your children will be unable to share or resolve with you, or with their friends. Young men especially find it hard to identify and share their feelings, and often resort to risk-taking – drinking, fighting or shoplifting – to work out their confusion.

I found a grief counsellor invaluable, both to keep me going and to help the children sort through the complex of their emotions. I was being too hard on myself, trying to be a perfect mother. In my concern to be responsible, and not let the tragedy damage their lives, I was offering conditional love – do well at school, stay out of trouble, be helpful, mature and understanding, and I'll love you. What they needed was constant and stable love – without strings. Their inner resources would eventually do the rest.

A guide to grief counselling services is included in Appendix A. Do contact one, with or without your children, if you would like to talk to someone with experience of bereavement, whose purpose is to comfort and assist you.

7

Food

A friend teased me that I couldn't write about anything without mentioning food. Probably true, but I don't apologise: we now accord a higher place to food than we used to, and for good reasons. Food comforts, relieves boredom, celebrates, expresses friendship or concern. It can also make the heaviest single demand on us. Every day, food must be organised and provided, even though our life has just fallen apart! You don't feel like eating anything, much less preparing it, yet you have to 'keep up your strength'. You really will get sick if you don't eat something nourishing.

This is where friends and family can help. (See also 'Friends and Family'.) A friend who had recently been bereaved knew exactly what to do: she arrived with several plastic freezer containers of a thick soup, which we steadily demolished in the next couple of weeks. Others brought soup, cakes, casseroles, a quiche. A young friend described the weeks after her mother's death as 'endless cups of tea'; and it's good to be able to offer something to eat to those who call to share your grieving.

You will probably not want to leave the house much for a while; and anyway when you get to the shop, you may not be able to think what to buy. Ask a friend to shop for you – lots of simple re-heatable food you can share with one or ten. For a while, it hardly matters that most of your food consists of instant meals.

Or you may have the opposite reaction, and go into

a frenzy of activity. After Rex died I had to be busy all the time, and a friend and I scrubbed the house from ceiling to skirting board. Had I been a cook, I might have found comfort in the kitchen. If this is you, prepare lots of food and freeze it (in a friend's freezer if you don't have one), for when your energy exhausts itself you will still need to eat!

And don't sneer at takeaway food, especially if there are young children to be fed. The home delivery firms are useful too (though expensive); don't feel awkward about letting friends pay for the odd meal if they are sharing it with you.

8

Correspondence

There are two kinds of letters to think about. The first kind is what you need to write, to acknowledge friends' sympathy and kindness, without adding another burden to your grief. The other, more painful and often longer-lasting, is the post which continues to arrive, addressed to your partner, sometimes taking you by surprise, and always rubbing salt into your wound.

Letters to Write

As soon as news spreads of your partner's death, many people will send their messages of support and consolation. Some will send flowers, others a personal letter in which they express not only their concern for you, but also their own sense of shock and loss. Yet others will send a note, or a card: many people cannot find words for their distress.

I have treasured all these messages, and opening my post became a personal ritual. I learned not to open letters and cards in company, but to save them until I could discreetly go to my room. Thoughtfully written words from a friend who shares some of your loss and pain can readily make you weep, even after you have managed to attain some composure during the day. A few weeks after Jack's death, I found these letters kept me in touch with my deepest feelings, when the day-to-day reality had begun to harden into a dull ache. I could often read them, cry for a while, and, feeling relieved, rejoin my family.

The problem, of course, is that you need to reply to all these kind friends, and this can seem impossible and overwhelming. Firstly, remember that in writing to you friends are meeting *their* need, to communicate their sadness and express their love for you. A few people may expect a prompt and full response, but most of your friends don't write in anticipation of a long, thoughtful reply. You should not think of sending them one, unless you want to. A friend found writing long letters after his wife's death was very helpful to him, in organising and even understanding his emotional reactions. But few people will respond in this way, and then only with certain close friends. For most of us, the effort required to write letters is beyond us for a long time.

Yet you will want to acknowledge their letters in some way. The simplest procedure is to buy packets of 'thank you' cards, and write your friend's name and yours. If you have family or friends to help you, they can address the envelopes. I kept two manila folders, one answered and one not yet answered. As an additional check on myself, since I did not feel very reliable, I ticked the corner of each card or letter as I replied to it. There were friends to whom I wanted to communicate more, but was incapable at this stage. I still sent them a simple 'thank you' card, adding 'I'll write properly soon'. I put their letters aside, already ticked; this eliminated for me a sense of urgency or obligation I might otherwise have endured. Some of those 'proper' letters were not written for months, but I had done what I felt was necessary, and that was enough. Could anyone who cares about you feel slighted by this solution? I hope not.

Many people have a card printed, and this can also serve as a memento of your partner, for your friends. In Appendix C, I include some ideas for the wording: any commercial printer will provide this service quite inexpensively; but do get a couple of quotes if cost is a concern for you.

Correspondence For Your Partner

Post which keeps arriving, addressed to your partner, will hurt you in several ways. It reminds you continually that your partner is no longer here. It emphasises the new reality: you now have sole responsibility for all the things you used to share – bills, banking, insurance policies, car registration, etc. It also creates a new area with which you have to cope – notifications of your partner's death, change of name on accounts, removal from mailing lists, including all those unsolicited computer-generated ones that keep appearing.

A lot of this can be dealt with quite simply, if you or a friend have access to a typewriter and a photocopier. I typed a couple of form letters (see Appendix D), and made a large number of copies. (A friend could do this from your draft. Typing and word-processing businesses will prepare letters for you, for a charge. Public and college libraries have photocopiers, as do many small shops.)

The joint accounts, and those in your partner's name, should be dealt with first. (See also 'Immediately'.) Occasionally, firms who have closed your partner's account send a letter or notice sometime later. ('A mistake' they say. 'His/her name is still in the computer.') I always ring the company immediately, putting into my voice my anger at their thoughtlessness. Computers don't send notices by themselves: people program and operate them. People who have been notified of the death, and have failed to stop that post, should know how hurt and angry their carelessness has made you.

Sometimes the odd personal letter arrives, from a

friend or acquaintance who has not heard. Don't feel you have to answer the letter, except by a simple note saying '... died on ... of a .... I'll write more fully soon.' Tick it, and file it, either with those 'dealt with', or with those you will write to more fully.

Then there are circulars and magazines. I put them in a pile, and once a week I took out my photocopies, wrote names and addresses on them, signed them and sent them off. Or you can sign a stack of form letters, and give the job to a friend or family member. Or deal with each day's post in this way as it arrives, if you are not a hardened procrastinator like me. Both Rex and Jack were on many mailing lists, but the task was not, in the end, too formidable. I did become annoyed when I knew that I had notified a journal, yet the next issue, or worse, request for a renewal, arrived at the regular time. Then I wrote in large letters across the front: 'Return to sender. Addressee deceased. Already notified' – and sent it back. I hoped there was at least one red face when it arrived back where it came from. Never mind their sensitivities. Did they think about yours?

In a couple of months, the stream of correspondence shrinks to a trickle, but keep a few photocopies on hand. Every so often, a circular will arrive, addressed to your partner, which has the capacity to catch you off guard. Try not to be hurt: large organisations and the duplication of mailing lists make it hard to track down and eliminate all copies of your partner's name and address. No one person or department can ensure that this is complete, so you will need to persevere. (I sent at least eight letters to different sections of one large publisher before I succeeded in stopping their mail to Jack.) It is understandable that you become angry at this continued invasion of your hard-earned peace of mind. Feel free to return it with a reproach on the envelope for everyone to see. Phone and let them know that they should be doing better. Some 'junk mail' has the power to wound.

Most importantly, try not to let the post create unnecessary pressure for you. Reply to everything which will drive you crazy if left unanswered: but keep it short and simple, and enlist help if you can. Remember that most of your friends know what you are going through, and want you to write to them (or ring them) only when you feel you can. There are some people who feel nervous when you suffer a loss, and anxious that they may lose your friendship as a result. They may wait for a call from you, to let them know that you still need them. You may decide to 'shelve' them for a while, if their demands on you seem unreasonable. Some friendships do not survive such a trauma; you do however discover the people who respond most readily and appropriately to your needs.

9

Possessions

When you have shared your life with someone who has died, there are physical reminders all around you. These range from their own possessions (clothes, books, personal items), through things you bought or collected together (ornaments, pictures), to all the aspects of the household (furnishings, garden, perhaps the house itself) which are the result of your joint labour and decision-making – in other words, your life together. Decisions about these things have profound implications, especially altering or disposing of some of them. You have to accept the finality of the loss: your partner no longer needs the clothes in the wardrobe, will never now read the books on the shelves. But you are not yet ready to acknowledge that finality; even if the death was expected, there is still a sense of unreality about it, which may persist for weeks, even months.

Give Yourself Time

Reactions to this situation vary enormously, and you have to feel your way. An important principle, however, is not to rush into decisions. Give yourself time to adapt to the new situation, don't feel you have to do anything immediately, wait until you feel ready to begin to let go.

At first I found comfort in leaving everything exactly as it was, the same clothes in the wardrobe, the ornaments and photos in the same place on the desk.

Sharing

If your partner knew they were going to die, they may have indicated a wish that particular friends and family members have a memento of their choosing. A friend wanted me to have a pair of her earrings, which I wear on special occasions with a feeling of deep gratitude for our friendship. Our closest Papua New Guinean friend, who had become part of the family, chose Rex's sandals to wear and remember him every day. I invited Jack's family to choose from his books; each selected one which had special meaning for them.

So long as the will leaves everything (or at least all 'personal effects') to you, there is no problem. However, if there is no will, or if it divides the estate between a number of people, you will need to be more careful. All personal effects have to be valued for probate, but it is probably all right to share things of no monetary value (e.g. family photos). If you are not sure, check this with a solicitor.

You can first remove, or reserve, anything you cannot bear to part with; it is important that in making a gesture of compassion for other people's grief you don't plant seeds for your own regret. Remember that you now have to live without the person most central to your life, and must find comfort in whatever ways you can.

On the other hand, extending your concern, showing that you recognise their pain, also comforts you. A circle of loving friends and family can provide immense support and comfort. Too many people lash out in their anger and pain, allowing a struggle to develop over possessions, and add to the sense of loss and despair that pervades a family when someone dies.

Finding Your Way

After Jack died, I left his clothes in the wardrobe, his slippers by the bed, his gown behind the door, and was comforted by seeing them there every morning. About six weeks later, as I began to accept his death, I realised that these constant reminders were beginning to depress me. I was trying to face the reality of life without him, but there were traces of his physical presence everywhere I turned. Yet I still couldn't decide to dispose of them – I hadn't yet reached *that* level of acceptance!

So I put them into two large suitcases on top of my wardrobe – out of sight, but still in the back of my mind. Months later still, I was able to go through them again, assure myself that I had taken out all the things I and the children wanted to keep and could now 'safely' let them go. I gave them to a needy cause he would have approved of, and, though sad, was satisfied. And I was grateful that my situation, and my previous experience, had allowed me the possibility of letting go gradually, and in my own time.

Other things – souvenirs, ornaments, books, papers – have to be dealt with; this can also be done in stages, whenever you feel capable of making another set of decisions. Try not to let well-meaning friends press you into quick decisions; or worse, make them for you.

Of course there are circumstances in which friends or family can decide, and you will welcome this. But be sure you make the decisions you want to make when you are ready to make them; things you cannot decide about can usually be stored for a while, either by friends or family, or even commercially if necessary.

Within days of Jack's death, I had gone through his most personal belongings, put aside the ones I needed to keep, and asked all the children to choose what they would like to have. (This must be done carefully, to avoid hurt and resentment if possible.) This sharing, though painful, was, I felt, worthwhile – we talked about our memories, shared recollections of situations and events, wept together, and came away each holding one or two articles which held a special memory of the man we loved.

Books and Other Collections

Many people leave collections which have had a particular meaning in their lives. In my experience, books have occupied this special place. But any collection can be a problem if its owner dies and you are left with the responsibility for disposing of it respectfully.

For people who work with books, the books themselves seem to take on a special meaning. People love their books, and having gained ideas, even understanding or occasionally wisdom from them, feel that books are among their most significant possessions.

The decision to keep or dispose of them may be difficult. If there are not too many, and especially if they reflect your shared interests, it is not a problem to keep them on the shelves, at least until you cannot afford the space. But if it is a large professional library, you may worry about the space they occupy, and wonder whether anyone will ever read most of them.

Rex's professional library was housed in his office at the university. When he knew he was going to die, he decided to give all those books to a young colleague for whom he had much affection and respect. I was happy with this, as the books would have a 'good home', and be loved and well-used.

Jack's books were more difficult. I was happy to keep the art, music and travel books, many of which were bought during our shared life. But the thousands of

Australian history books would mostly sit gathering dust, I feared.

A friend suggested donating them to a new university about to be established. Wonderful! They would stay together (mostly), and would be welcome and well-used. And possibly they could even have a book-plate in each of them in Jack's memory.

Another friend told me about a special taxation scheme, which enabled me to donate the books as I wanted, and claim the value as a tax benefit.

This was complicated, since I had to arrange for two valuations of the collection; yet it proved to be a warming experience. Both valuers were booklovers who admired the collection and, in doing so, were also approving Jack's knowledge of the literature of his subject. Indeed, one of them said after a careful examination: 'I like your husband! He had a wonderful library'.

Pleased as I was with this solution, it was still heart-wrenching to let the books go. They were so much part of Jack and our life together – moving, packing, unpacking, arranging, buying new bookshelves to accommodate them all. I was glad I was at work when they came to collect them. The shelves were sadly empty when I came home that night.

The Bed

The bed you have shared with your partner can be a source of concern. It is where you have shared most intimacy, and is perhaps the only place you have shared exclusively with your partner. Immediately after their death, you may find it very difficult to sleep in the large empty bed by yourself, and may either move into another bed, or allow small children to share it with you. It is especially hard if your partner died in the bed, as the memories are sharp and the associations painful.

Returning to your marriage bed, on your own, is another step towards accepting your partner's death, and your new status as a single person. This is particularly important if you have the possibility of developing a new relationship; in any event once you have conquered your nervousness you can feel satisfied with this small act of courage.

Accepting Change

Even harder perhaps than deciding about individual items, is to make decisions about the house – to move the furniture, change the furnishings or, hardest of all, to sell up and move away. What makes a house your home is the memories stored in it: the stain on the carpet from the first teenage party, the shelf your partner put up, the sofa you saved for and bought together in triumph, the rosebushes you planted or the rock wall you built. Everyone has a list like this, of things done together; and another, of things yet to be done, in the shared future that death has just swept away.

It is tempting to make your home a museum, a mausoleum even, where everything must remain as it was when your partner was alive. To move the pictures around, to paint the bedroom a different colour, seems disloyal and insensitive to the memory of your partner.

Yet life does go on, and those feelings of disloyalty will assault you in many areas of your life, especially as it begins to return to something like 'normal'. The first time you really laugh, the first day you don't wake up remembering, the first outing you enjoy with a friend, you will feel a twinge of guilt that life could begin to feel good again. But it is an inevitable and essential part of healing. And heal you must, if the rest of your life is not to be a pale shadow of what it could still be.

You will never forget your partner, or the meaning of

your life together. He or she is part of you, and of the lives of your family and friends. You are all changed, because of the person you have known and loved. Your partner will live on in all of you, and would want you all to go on living full and meaningful lives.

Sadly, especially at first, this means accepting the need to change aspects of your life, including your home. You will know when you are ready to make these decisions; don't push yourself. And remember that the most valuable and lasting mementoes of one you have loved are in yourself, your head and your heart.

Rex and I had lived in Port Moresby, and there was a strong Papua New Guinean feel to our house. Jack must have been keenly aware of this, but lived with and accepted it for a long time before he judged that I was ready to let go of that part of my past, and replace 'Rex's and my' pictures and hangings with some representing 'Jack's and my' life together.

Letting Go

When you are finally able to 'let go' of something, it can give you immense relief and even freedom.

Jack was a committed collector, of just about everything. So a long stay overseas saw us return with a collection, not only of books, pamphlets and photographs, but also every imaginable bus and museum ticket, theatre and concert programme and review, invitation, and other piece of memorabilia. They were to be put into scrapbooks, which we bought; indeed Jack had completed one before he died. The rest sat on the floor in boxes, reproaching and oppressing me. When would I ever find time to carry out his wish to have a scrapbook collection of our trip?

Then, one remarkable day, I was struck by the idea that I didn't have to do it. That was Jack's thing, but it certainly wasn't mine! I gave up collecting theatre tickets 20 years ago. Since he was gone, I could THROW THEM ALL AWAY! I was elated, but nervous. Could I? Would it be disloyal? Hurtful? To whom? Not Jack – he was no longer here. Certainly not to me – I was feeling freer than I had since he died. But I let the idea simmer for some days before I was sure that it was right. And it was weeks before I actually did anything. Then one long weekend, when I was feeling cheerful and confident, I tackled the task. Box by box, I went through every item, re-living each occasion, remembering. I shed the odd tear, but also smiled at the good times we shared, now that the pain had receded far enough to be able to have 'happy memories'. And I threw it almost all away, keeping only the very occasional, especially significant piece.

The line between keeping and discarding is different for everyone, and also at different stages in your grieving and healing. But if you only throw away what you are certain you can let go of, you can always come back later and do it again. Progressively it hurts less, as your wounds heal. It is hard, and requires considerable emotional energy, but it can be comforting to remember and re-live parts of your life together in this way, however long after your partner's death.

10

Fatigue

You feel continually tired for quite a long time, and I think you need to accept this, and learn to live with it. There are two basic reasons:

Sleep

First, you will probably find it very difficult to sleep, for as soon as you close your eyes memories of your partner come flooding in and swirl around in your mind. They may be happy or sad memories, but as everything you remember about your life together is painful, it all has the same effect of emphasising your loneliness and loss. For six months after Rex died, I woke up early every morning with the scene of his death vividly in my mind. For reasons I discuss later, it was an intensely lonely and frightening experience which hovered around the edge of my consciousness for a very long time. When Jack died suddenly, the shock seemed to reverberate through my brain, keeping me awake through the night for many weeks, with only the occasional snatch of sleep.

Exhausting Emotions

Second, and a longer-term problem, the emotions you are experiencing – grief, anger, guilt, sadness, hurt, loneliness, frustration, anxiety, panic attacks – sap your energy and drain your usual ability to cope, even in quite ordinary situations. Getting a meal together is an effort that often seems beyond you. (Here is something friends and family can help with – allow them, ask them if you know them well enough, to shop for your basic food needs; to bring takeaways if they are coming to see you around mealtime.) While you don't want to be organised or pushed around, you may find it impossibly difficult to make decisions. Others will need to find ways of assisting you, suggesting alternatives and even solutions. Take the help you want; but be prepared to express your needs when you can identify them. I think it is very important not to be rushed into decisions you are not ready to make, and which do not have to be made yet.

When Rex died, I kept going, as in some ways I was prepared for his death. (You are never truly prepared, and cannot expect to be; even if you know someone is dying, you cannot predict the myriad ways in which you are going to miss him or her, or the intensity of your feelings.) Four months after his death, the kids and I went camping with friends, and I asked not to have to make a single decision. A month after that, we stayed with other friends. I took the kids to the beach, did almost nothing else, and slept twelve hours a day for a week. Rather like an illness, bereavement has physical effects from which you recover only slowly.

How To Get Some Rest

People approach this problem in different ways. Think about getting up and doing something; lying there going over the same events, emotions, anxieties in your mind is the most depressing and incapacitating experience you can have.

Whether or not you go back to work at once, it is useful to nap whenever you can. Be prepared to go to bed late and/or get up early. Try to find things to do while you are reluctantly awake, which let you focus on something else. After Jack died, I found sleep almost impossible, so I napped on the living-room couch, with the television on and the sound barely audible. Night after night I dozed in and out of the all-night American news programmes, the voices of Irangate commentators punctuating my despair. For many months I often woke early, and my thoughts went immediately to Jack. I think I frequently woke from dreaming about him, though I rarely remembered the dreams. I found it best to listen to the radio (talking – music is not distracting enough for me, though perhaps it is for you) till I (usually) drifted off again.

Sleeping pills and other tranquillisers should be discussed with your doctor. I have tried to avoid the use of drugs. However, friends have found some to be helpful, indeed necessary for a while, just to get enough sleep to be able to cope at all with a day at a time. A gentler alternative is a glass of warm milk before you go to bed (if you like warm milk – or hot chocolate, or try it with whisky).

The trouble with tranquillisers is that they are addictive. When you have little strength or energy it is tempting to depend on them to get some sleep. But they are a solution only to short-term problems which can be resolved in a matter of days. For example, the night before the funeral, you may feel you desperately need enough sleep to be able to cope with the next day. Then take a sleeping pill for that particular purpose. But you need to realise that as soon as you don't take one, you will probably not sleep, and it may take a long time for your body to adjust to the enormous stress it is now under.

Some doctors feel awkward about not being able to 'fix' your pain. So be wary of one who freely prescribes pills as a way in which he or she can deal with their sense of inadequacy, rather than your grief. Of course you feel depressed, since you have a very good reason. Antidepressants (or 'happy' pills) may make everyone around you feel better, since something is 'being done' to deal with your unhappiness; but it is no solution for you. You will need to experience your feelings of sadness and loss in order to come to terms with them, and your family and friends (and even your doctor) will have to accept this.

Deadening the Pain

Some people also use pills or alcohol to deaden the pain of loss. I once said to a friend that I wished I could just keep drinking, to maintain the numbing semi-stupor we see in Hollywood films when the hero suffers such a loss. I would like to suspend myself in an alcoholic haze somewhere above the terrible reality. 'No', he said, 'it doesn't work. All it does is postpone the realisation and the anguish. You have to go through it eventually.' He then told me that this was how he had behaved when his wife died, and how much longer it had consequently taken him to accept her death and address his grief.

An additional problem with alcohol is that it is a depressant. Since first it depresses our inhibitions, we feel good after a few drinks, and our sadness may lift for a while. It also helps friends who are feeling awkward about your loss, and may make conversation easier. (I think the great merit of ex-soldiers' reunions is the opportunity they give to otherwise constrained men to share their memories and their grief in a socially acceptable way.)

If this is the way you have reacted to previous crises, you will probably need alcohol now. It would be absurd for you to expect to behave 'perfectly' when you have just had such a loss. However alcohol *is* a depressant, and soon you may feel even worse. Try to control your drinking, so as not to punish yourself further. Some people find that if they can give themselves two or three days at a time with no alcohol, they notice that they feel better on those days.

My strong feeling is that grief is a tunnel in an enormous mountain: there is no way round, only through. The more openly and honestly you acknowledge your loss and your pain, the more you share it with family and friends and allow them to help you, the more readily you accept your fatigue and your reduced capacity to cope, the more quickly (however slowly it seems at the time) and completely you will be able to dig your way through the tunnel, and out into the sunshine on the other side!

11

Helping to Die

When your partner is terminally ill, many questions arise about the nature of the event called death. How will it occur? When? How much notice will we have? How will we recognise it? Perhaps most pressingly of all, how much pain will the dying person have to endure, and how can we help?

People vary enormously in their desire to know the answers, and even in their ability to frame the questions. At one extreme is the woman whose husband was in the same ward as Rex. She 'did not know' that her husband had cancer. She declined to notice that her husband was a patient in a cancer ward, or that his strength persistently faded, and resolutely asked no questions of the doctors or nurses. We must assume that there are people who systematically (though perhaps unconsciously) avoid this kind of knowledge. Others press their doctors for exact dates and times of death, precise details the doctors themselves cannot possibly know. You can push away a lot of these issues in coping with the day-to-day needs of your sick partner. However, sooner or later, in many terminal illnesses pain becomes a concern.

Pain

There are at least three ways of dealing with the pain of a dying person. The first (and for me the least acceptable) is to regard the pain as an unavoidable and untreatable condition of the illness, and simply let it occur, eased from time to time by fairly arbitrarily prescribed pain-killers, and controlled in essence by doctors and not by those living with the pain. This is now a very outdated response to terminal pain. If it is your doctor's attitude, I can only suggest that you challenge that attitude, or change your doctor.

Palliative Care and Hospice Home Care

Palliative care (also known as hospice home care) is being widely adopted. Palliative care aims not to cure, but to make people comfortable and free of pain. Therefore palliative care nursing provides physical, social and emotional support for dying patients and their families. Its philosophy is to give people greater control over their well-being, alleviating unnecessary pain and distress, and easing the dying process for individuals and their families. For information about obtaining palliative care, see Appendix G.

Pamela, whose leukaemia had become acute, joined a palliative care programme. This meant a number of things to her and her care-giving family. First, they acknowledged that Pamela would probably die, and that there was little prospect of a medical cure. Second, although she would seek and accept medical intervention to improve the quality of her life, there would come a time when she would refuse further hospitalisation, and die with dignity in her own home.

She wore a syringe-driver, which automatically gave small and frequent injections of morphine. This device enabled her to live at home. She entertained and went out with friends when she wished, and was more independent than she had been as a hospital patient.

This kind of care ranges from telephone contact to regular visits from specialist palliative care nurses. Pamela's nurses came twice daily to dispense the morphine, help meet the difficult physical needs such as showering and using the toilet, and bring invaluable cheer, encouragement and support to the whole family. They accepted the likelihood of Pamela's death, so they were able to discuss it honestly with her. Their professional skill as nurses and as explainers of new symptoms put her family at ease with day-to-day developments, and allayed their fear of the unexpected, which might have alarmed them.

As the disease intensified, the morphine dose was gradually increased so that she often dozed off, or seemed to float a little above the reality around her. Yet she remained with and close to those she loved, who were able to give her the constant care and comfort she needed, which every loving family wants to provide. She died in her own bed, with her husband and children, without pain and without fear. She had achieved an understanding of herself, her world, and the completeness of living and dying which have become an example of courage and dignity to everyone who shared her experience.

Pamela's care depended on many unusual circumstances: her extraordinary capacity to deal honestly and openly with each stage of her illness, including her approaching death; a grown-up family with the financial freedom to devote most of their time to her; a large and pleasant house to accommodate many visitors at once; and ready access to a palliative care service.

Few people will have all these advantages, but an increasing number will be able to make some use of this new and humane development in the health services.

Helping to Die

The most difficult – and as yet illegal – way of all is to assist the dying person to take their own life, even to administer the dose when, for example, they may not physically be able to do it themselves. Euthanasia ('mercy killing' as it is often called) is controversial and, in the United Kingdom, illegal. Yet it *is* merciful, and in many circumstances when one you love is going to die, and is in great pain and distress, it may seem the only act available to you to deliver them from further suffering. Thus many people think of acting in this way, and it would be cowardly to evade it here.

My father found himself dying slowly of emphysema. He discharged himself from hospital, to die quietly among friends. He swallowed what he thought would be a fatal dose of chloroquin, but could not keep it down, and was re-admitted to hospital. Although he did finally manage to obtain a sufficient quantity of sleeping tablets to achieve his purpose, he was outraged by his lack of control over his own life and death.

Rex's cancer began in the lung, and travelled quickly to his spine and then to his brain. He found the physical pain, intense though it often was, tolerable. What was intolerable was the prospect that a proud, intelligent and controlled man could feel his mental capacity disintegrate, and be powerless to end his life when it became meaningless and abhorrent to him. Long before anyone else was aware of it, he noticed that his speech was beginning to blur, and that he could not always put his tongue to the precise word he wanted. He greatly feared losing his dignity, indeed 'losing his mind', so we talked about how his life could be ended when *he* chose, when he felt it could no longer give him enough of what he wanted from it.

An understanding doctor visited us at home, and talked about 'quality of life', and about not prolonging life without meaning. He said he agreed with us, and would be there to help us when Rex felt the time had come. But because of the (then) illegality of suicide, and the (continuing) illegality of assisting suicide, the risks, and his real fear of losing his right to practise medicine, he seemed to us to talk in riddles. Little was actually said, though much was hinted at. We remained anxious and uncertain about what would eventually happen.

Rex hung on bravely, and even came home for Christmas which, though painfully sad for us, seemed to comfort the children. By Boxing Day, though, he wished his life to end quickly, while he still felt a whole person, both to himself and to his family. He went back into hospital, and I will never forget the anguish of driving behind the ambulance, knowing that this was the beginning of his final journey out of our lives.

Within a day or two, having been taken off all medication at his own request, but facing the prospect of lingering for at least some weeks, he took a large dose of sleeping pills. We said our final farewells, I sat with him until he dozed off, and went home to await the inevitable call from the hospital to tell me he had died in his sleep.

Except that it didn't come. After a long sleepless night I phoned the ward, to be told by a cheerful sister that he had slept well and was eating his breakfast! By the time I reached the hospital he was distraught, confused and slightly incoherent, but absolutely clear that he shouldn't still be here.

We held hands through the day. I didn't let the children visit, as they had already seen him for the last time as he wanted to be remembered. That night, New Year's Eve, I knew I had to try again. The friendly doctor had prescribed sleeping pills for me, and indicated what would be a lethal dose. But the pills were only half the strength he said they would be, so did Rex need twice as many? Who could I ask? Our doctor was on leave. To whom could I entrust the guilty secret that Rex wanted his life to end, and that as he now clearly needed help, I was willing to help him. No one. We were on our own. Fourteen years later, I still feel the rage and despair of being abandoned in our urgent need. That a beloved partner has to die is enough to bear; that enabling him or her to die with dignity should be accompanied by such terror and helplessness is an outrage in a society that considers itself civilised or caring.

By now he was too confused to take the pills by himself, so I fed them to him. Fearful of failing again, but not knowing the appropriate dose, I gave him as many pills as he could swallow. I kissed him, and then read him 'to sleep'. I was terrified but determined to see it through.

I don't know when he died. I have no medical training and had no experience of death. Was the breathing noise that seemed to come from his chest the 'death rattle' I had heard of, but didn't understand? Was the pulse I felt for in his throat his or mine? I tried putting a mirror to his lips – was I doing it properly? How would I know?

So I sat, heart in mouth, holding his hand (still warm), reading. Until the midnight hospital round, and a sister who *did* know how to tell felt for his pulse and found nothing.

Even then it was not over. I was expelled from the room while a doctor was summoned. Would they try to revive him? Pump his stomach? Was it finished for him yet? I burst into the room, begging them to let him be; he wanted to die. He had died and they didn't try to resuscitate him; for Rex it was finally over.

As for me, I still had to engage wih a young and inexperienced doctor. I refused a post-mortem, and became angry when he tried to persuade me to sign the papers. 'Standard hospital procedure', he said and, I'm afraid to say, got an earful about standard hospital procedures from a frightened but very determined young widow. Eventually I went home, not yet to grieve, but to lie awake waiting for the police to knock on my door and arrest me for murder.

Committing suicide, which was illegal in Australia when Rex died, is now legal both in Australia and in the United Kingdom. That is, a person is now legally allowed to take his or her own life. But assisting, aiding and abetting, or counselling to procure a suicide is still illegal, and punishable by up to 14 years imprisonment. Of course in reality a seriously ill person is not always able to act independently, however much they desire to end their life.

How long will it be before the law-makers and moral standard-bearers of our society have the courage and honesty to allow terminally ill people the right to choose to die with dignity? How long before they remove from loving friends and family the responsibility for helping their loved ones to die, and place it in the hands of professional care-givers, who have the knowledge and the means to end life humanely and responsibly?

Of course there must be ways of guarding against abuse. Certainly there are religious prohibitions which must operate, and be respected, for individuals. But we have begun to question the definition of 'life' as minimal bodily function. We talk about 'quality' of life, and begin to understand that there is some kind of life which those who have it feel is no longer worth the struggle.

Some countries have begun to move towards legalising voluntary euthanasia, and there is certainly widespread public support for this. In Britain advice and information can be obtained from the Voluntary Euthanasia Society (though the law does not allow them to advise you how to commit suicide). The preparation of an advance directive (or living will) requesting only palliative care is now popular; its legal force is being investigated by a House of Lords enquiry. The guidelines under which Dutch doctors have been able to practise active voluntary euthanasia for some years have now been formalised in law. In Switzerland and Germany physician-assisted suicide is legal. In Western Europe and North America, voluntary euthanasia is widely discussed. As with other moral issues, public opinion will play a great part in urging law-makers to meet this growing need.

Talking About It

It is so hard to talk about death and dying in our society that many people avoid it altogether. When someone you love is diagnosed as having a terminal illness, you feel you are admitting defeat to talk about how and when they will die. You want to keep their (and your) spirits up, to hope for a miracle (which sometimes does happen), so you can't raise the issue of whether and when they would wish to take control of their dying.

But at some stage it will become possible to ask the questions, to give them the chance to express their wishes. Dying people often accept this reality long before those who will survive them. Many have written of not raising these issues out of concern for their care-givers, 'so as not to frighten or depress them'. It does take courage to discuss these concerns, but once the barrier is down, you have the chance of a new and deeper understanding.

Of course some dying people don't want to face these issues, and their wishes must be respected. But more often we don't give them a choice, and this must make them feel even more frightened and isolated.

If your partner is chronically ill, think about how to raise these issues. A question like 'Do you want to talk about dying?' can be answered either way with a word. A discussion with your doctor, a hospital psychologist, social worker, counsellor, or sympathetic friend will help you to clarify your attitudes and feelings, and assist you to handle the concerns of your partner most reassuringly.

If you and your partner feel no need to consider the issues I have raised in this chapter, of course that is your choice and your right. But please think about the assumptions you may have made yourself, and try to give the person you love the freedom to talk with you about their death, which to a dying person inevitably at some point becomes the focus of their life.

12

Will I Ever Be Really Happy Again?

A year to the day after Jack died, I experienced the feeling that I might soon begin to enjoy life again. I had spent a gruelling few days, trying to get away on a holiday we all needed. We spent four hours in a cold, wet, windy bus shelter praying that Michael's flu would not become pneumonia. We endured crossed wires, missed connections, and continual spirit-dampening rain.

Yet, at the end of the journey, the sun appeared brilliantly and set most beautifully behind the mountains, across the water. Perhaps, I thought as I strode along the sand, it is a symbol; perhaps I am again ready for the sun to shine in my life. I do not hold with signs and portents from outside ourselves. But I do believe we must take what life gives us, seize it with both hands, and make the best we can of it.

Until then, I had kept going for the sake of my family and my work. Dinner on the table (most evenings anyway!) to maintain order and normality, hard work into the night to ward off loneliness and the exhausting re-living of painful memories, giving to my family and friends to try to make some sense of it all, not wanting anything for myself beyond getting through each day, and waiting impatiently for the pain to subside.

Grief is different for each of us. We find different ways of coping with the emotional and practical burdens. Much depends on our experiences and our support system. We require distinct kinds of assistance, and respond differently to offers of help.

I hope that my experiences have helped you to feel that you are not alone. Many of us who have lost a partner have worked through our grieving, and feel able to face life again with hope, even relish. You will not forget your partner or your life together. You may sometimes feel sad or lonely, but eventually it is possible to accept your loss in a way which allows you to live a full and meaningful life. Your life has not ended with your partner's.

You may meet someone with whom you will be happy to share your life again. If you make that decision, you risk losing a partner again, being terribly hurt. Yet you also choose to share your life with someone who loves you. You choose joy and laughter, warmth and caring.

Many who have lost a partner, especially a life-long one, will not consider another intimate relationship. This does not mean that you will never be happy again. Happiness and love are available to us in many areas of our lives – sharing with friends, the laughter of children, the beauty of a sunrise (or a sunset if, like me, you have trouble getting up early!), the joy of giving, the delight of helping someone do something they hadn't thought possible.

You could make your own list of things that please you. If it is very short right now, as it surely will be if you have just lost someone you love, try the checklist I include at the back of the book (Appendix B).

Time does heal, but grief seems to need such a lot of time, and perhaps you are feeling, as I have felt, that time will never pass, that you ought to feel less devastated now than you do – I found the seeming endlessness of that misery frustrating and hard to bear. You may feel that others are weary of your unhappiness, and you ought to be 'doing better'.

All I can say is: I know how that feels, and it takes much longer than anyone wants it to, but someday the cloud *will* lift, and you will feel a bit better. Then it drops again, crushingly, but soon it will lift again, each time for a little longer. And someday you will again feel that life is worth living. Good luck!

Epilogue

When Pamela died, her husband Donald and I spent a lot of time in each other's company. We had shared much anguish during her illness, and found comfort in each other's understanding. It was often easier to talk to each other than to friends who had not lost a partner, or kept so closely in touch with the stages of Pamela's illness.

We had been friends for a long time with each other and our partners. This made it comfortable to share our memories. Our children were the same ages and we found common ground in their responses to the tragedies in their lives. We were both single parents with responsibilities it was good to talk about. Soon we fell in love.

I found this wonderful and frightening. Was I taking advantage of his vulnerability? Was I getting into a new relationship before I was ready, simply because I needed to be loved? Could I bear the pain if anything unpleasant happened to him or to us? Yet his warmth was magical. We both needed to be cherished and cared for, we enjoyed each other's company, we gave each other hope of new happiness. How could this be wrong?

It often happens that people who have supported each other through a tragedy fall in love. Meeting each other's deepest needs is an excellent foundation for a lasting relationship. Yet we also feel more guilty. Will our children be hurt? or outraged? or both? Does this seem to them the ultimate betrayal of their parents' friendships? Will others assume we have taken advantage of a tragic situation for our own purposes? Who will be shocked, and how important is that to us?

These were real questions for us, and we pondered them deeply for a long time. Children's feelings are particularly important, and we must be sensitive and tactful. They need time to adjust to new situations, and to feel that their reactions are worthy of our consideration and understanding. Having taken all this into account, however, we must do what seems right for us.

Donald and I are now married, and are very happy together. He has helped me enormously. I hope I have helped him to keep Pamela alive in all our memories, and to let her go. We cannot know what lies in our future, and I think that is just as well. Despite my apprehension, I look forward to it.

Appendix A:
Bereavement Counselling Services
and Helpful Organisations

Bereavement Counselling Services

General
Hospitals
Most large hospitals offer grief or bereavement counselling. Enquire through the hospital chaplain or social worker.

Telephone
Cruse Bereavement Line, business hours, Tel: 0181 332 7227. For 24-hour telephone counselling in your area, the Samaritans operate throughout Britain; local contacts listed in the front of the telephone book. Head office Tel: 01753 53 2713; Fax: 01753 81 9004.

Local Health Authorities
Your local health authority may refer you to a counsellor. Ask about cost when you are given the details.

Funeral Companies
Many funeral companies offer bereavement support and education services. These include short-term grief counselling, and brochures, books, tapes and videos.

These services are usually free. Contact your local funeral director (listed in the Yellow Pages), or the National Association of Funeral Directors, 618 Warwick Road, Solihull, West Midlands B91 1AA. Tel: 0121 711 1343.

Private Counsellors
Your local GP can refer you to a private counsellor, if your needs go beyond normal bereavement counselling. The British Association for Counselling, 1 Regent Place, Rugby, Warwicks CV21 2PJ; Tel: 01788 57 8328; Fax: 01788 56 2189, maintains a register of private counsellors, and can give you details

in your area. However, you do have to pay for these consultations.

Specialist Organisations
Age Concern England
Astral House, 1268 London Road, London SW16 4ER. Tel: 0181 679 8000.
Promotes effective care and well-being of older people, positive attitudes to ageing. Produces many publications and fact sheets. Local telephone numbers and addresses in the phone book.

Cruse Bereavement Care
Cruse House, 126 Sheen Road, Richmond, Surrey TW9 1UR. Tel: 0181 940 4818.
Provides a national service of bereavement counselling, advice and information, and social contact. Has 195 branches throughout the United Kingdom; listed in phone books and Thomson's Directories. Operates a bereavement line during business hours, Tel: 0181 332 7227. Local groups offer all kinds of help, including pastoral visiting, small group support, counselling.

Help the Aged
St James's Walk, London EC1R 0BE. Tel: 0171 253 0253.
Produce a leaflet called *Bereavement*, which gives emotional and practical advice.

Jewish Bereavement Counselling Service
1 Cyprus Gardens, London N3 1SP. Tel: 0171 387 4300 ext 227; 0181 349 0839 (24-hour answerphone).
Offers emotional support and assistance to bereaved Jewish people and information about Jewish bereavement customs. Free bereavement counselling in London area by trained counsellors.

Lesbian and Gay Bereavement Project
Vaughan M. Williams Centre, Colindale Hospital, London
NW9 5HG. Tel: 0181 455 8894 (helpline); 0181 200 0511
(admin).
Provides advice and support for bereaved gay men and
women, practical help in London with funeral arrangements
etc. Send s.a.e. for a simple will form to use in gay
partnerships.

National Association of Bereavement Services
20 Norton Folgate, London E1 6DB. Tel: 0171 247 0617
(admin); 0171 247 1080 (referrals); Fax: 0171 247 3436.
Promotes awareness of bereavement issues, information about
training; offers telephone referral advice on services throughout the United Kingdom. Publishes *Directory of Bereavement
and Loss*, updated annually, £75.

Life-threatening Illnesses

ACET (Aids Care, Education and Training)
PO Box 1323, Ealing W5 5TF. Tel: 0181 840 7879; Fax: 0181
840 2616.
Provides home care support, education and training throughout the UK and Ireland.

Bacup
3 Bath Place, Rivington Street, London EC2A 3JR. Tel: 0171
613 2121; 0800 181199 (information – freeline for callers
from outside London); 0171 696 9000 (counselling). Offers
information, advice and emotional support to cancer patients,
families and friends. Free, easy-to-understand publications on
types of cancer.

Cancerlink
17 Britannia Street, London WC1X 9JN. Tel: 0171 833 2818
(self-help and support service, admin); Fax: 0171 833 4963.
Provides emotional support and information on cancer. Publications on emotional and practical issues about cancer.

Hospice Information Service

51–59 Lawrie Park Road, Sydenham, London SE26 6DZ. Tel: 0181 778 9252; Fax: 0181 659 8680.

Offers information and support by telephone, business hours. It publishes a free annual directory of hospice services in the UK and Ireland; send an 11 × 9 inch stamped self-addressed envelope.

Marie Curie Cancer Care

28 Belgrave Square, London SW1X 8QG. Tel: 0171 235 3325. Advisory and nursing service for cancer patients and relatives, research and education. Operates terminal homes throughout the UK.

Voluntary Euthanasia Society

13 Prince of Wales Terrace, London W8 5PG. Tel: 0171 937 7770.

Promotes changes to legislation which will enable people to choose to die with dignity. They publish a newsletter, and provide members with information about their rights (and lack of rights). They also distribute advance directives and emergency medical treatment cards on request. An advance directive enables a person to request that medical intervention in a terminal illness or accident be limited to palliative care. An emergency medical treatment card (which you carry with you) notifies that you have made an advance directive, and gives the name and address of the doctor with whom it is lodged.

General Practical Assistance

Citizens' Advice Bureaux

Throughout the UK; listed in the telephone book. Can provide an enormous amount of practical assistance, eg advice about benefits, funeral expenses, drafting a will, help in applying for emergency funds.

Department of Social Security

Your local office provides advice about entitlements and assistance filling out the forms. Free publications include:

D49 *What to do after a death* – excellent summary of necessary tasks and sources of assistance.

FB29 *Help when someone dies: a guide to Social Security benefits.*

Local Authorities

Social workers in the Social Services Department of your local Borough or County Council can help you with many practical problems. Contact them at your local Town or County Hall.

Directories

Directory of Hospice Services in the UK and Republic of Ireland. Hospice Information Service, 51–59 Lawrie Park Road, Sydenham, London SE26 6DZ. Tel: 0181 778 9252; Fax: 0181 659 8680.

The Voluntary Agencies Directory. National Council for Voluntary Organisations, 26 Bedford Square, London WC1B 3HU. Tel: 0171 713 6161.

Appendix B:
We All Need Laughter

Here is a list of things most commonly found to cheer up depressed people. I hope some of them will work for you:

laughing
being relaxed
being with happy people
eating good meals
thinking about something good in the future
people showing interest in what you have said
thinking about people you like
seeing beautiful scenery
breathing clean air
being with friends
peace and quiet
being noticed as sexually attractive
kissing
hugging
watching people
frank and open conversations
sitting in the sun
wearing clean clothes
having spare time
doing a project in your own way
sleeping soundly at night
listening to music
having sexual relations
smiling at people
being told you are loved
reading stories, novels, poems or plays
planning or organising something
going to a restuarant
expressing love to someone
being with someone you love
seeing good things happen to your family or friends
complimenting or praising someone

having coffee, tea or a drink with friends
meeting someone new
driving skilfully
saying something clearly
being with animals
being popular at a gathering
planning trips or vacations
listening to the radio
learning a new skill
seeing old friends
watching wild animals
doing a job well
being asked for help or advice
amusing people
being complimented or told you have done well
jogging or other physical exercise

This list is freely adapted from P. Lewinsohn and J. Libet, 'Pleasant events, activity schedules, and depressions' in *Journal of Abnormal Psychology*, vol. 79, no. 3 (1972), pp. 291–5.

Appendix C:
Printed Cards

This is a standard small printing job for commercial printers (listed in the Yellow Pages). Phone a couple to get quotes, as they vary quite a lot. Ask whether they have standard forms, or whether they are happy to work from your design/wording.

Here are some ideas for wording:

(*Names of family members*) would like to express our sincere appreciation for thoughts, kindness and sympathy shown to us at the time of our recent sad bereavement.

Thank you for your thoughts.
They mean a great deal to us.
(*Names of family members*)

When I am gone, fear not to say my name,
Nor speak of me in muted tones
As if it were a shame for one to die,
But let me figure in your daily talk,
Tell of my loves and hates,
Of how I used to laugh, or want a walk;
That way, you'll keep me in your memory.
(*Names of family members*) thank you for your expressions of sympathy.

Appendix D:
Form Letters

(*Address*)
(*Space for date – write in as needed*)

Dear Madam/Sir,
I wish to inform you that (*name of your partner*) died on (*date*).
(*Space to add another sentence if necessary*)
Yours faithfully,

(*Your name*)

* * * * * *

(*Address*)
(*Space for date*)

Dear Madam/Sir,
This is to inform you that (*name of your partner*) died on (*date*). Please remove his/her name from your mailing list.
Yours faithfully,

(*Your name*)

* * * * *

(*Address*)
(*Space for date*)

The Manager/Credit Manager
(*Department Store/Gas/Electricity/Insurance Co/etc – leave space and write in as needed*)

Dear Madam/Sir,
My husband/wife/partner (*name of partner*) has had the following account/policy ———— (*give number etc*) with you.

I regret to inform you that he/she died on (*date*).

Would you kindly transfer the account to my name – and (*as necessary – leave space and write in*) issue a new card in my name/issue the appropriate amendment to my insurance policy/read the meter, charge the outstanding account to the estate of ——————— and open a new account in my name/ etc.

Thank you.

Yours faithfully,

(*Your name*)

Appendix E:
Funerals

Cremation

Cremation Society of Great Britain
Brecon House, Albion Place, Maidstone, Kent ME14 5DZ.
Tel: 01622 68 8292/3; Fax: 01622 68 6698.
Provides free information on all aspects of cremation, including a leaflet called *What you should know about cremation.*

General Information

National Association of Funeral Directors
618 Warwick Road, Solihull, West Midlands B91 1AA. Tel:
0121 711 1343; Fax: 0121 711 1351.
Provides information about funerals. Publishes a number of useful booklets:

> *Why?*
> *Health and Safety in the Funeral Service*
> *Perfect Assurance Funeral Trust*
> *Code of Practice (NAFD)*
> *A Loved One Dies*
> *Funerals: Care, Concern, Compassion*
> *The Role of the Funeral Director.*

Pre-arranged Funerals

A pre-arranged funeral allows you to pay your funeral expenses in advance, and to make all the decisions about the funeral service.

Payment is made to your local funeral director, at today's prices. The money is held in trust by the National Association of Funeral Directors, and there is no further cost.

Decisions you will need to make include:

cremation or burial;
church, cemetery chapel, crematorium chapel, or graveside
service;
content of funeral service;
type of coffin;
flowers or donations to specified charity;
any other details you feel strongly about.

Information may be obtained from any funeral director. If
necessary, contact the National Association of Funeral Directors (details above).

Appendix F:
Some Useful Books

Butler, Sandra, and Rosenblum, Barbara, *Cancer in Two Voices*. The Women's Press, London, 1994.

A powerful and moving account of a lesbian couple living with cancer. Needs concentration; perhaps more accessible some time before or after a close death.

Hastings, Diana, *Crisis Point: a Survivor's Guide to Living*. Papermac, London, 1989.

Comprehensive guide to life's crises and how to handle them. Includes large 'Help Directory' with invaluable information and contact list.

Jones, Mary, *Secret Flowers: Mourning and the adaptation to loss*. The Women's Press, London, 1988.

A gentle, moving account of the author's husband's death, and what she learned in coming to terms with her loss.

What To Do When Someone Dies: the Practical Arrangements That Have To Be Made After a Death. Revised edition. Consumers' Association and Penguin, London, 1994.

Helps anyone faced with making practical arrangements following a death. Easy-to-follow charts guide you through the necessary procedures.

Wills and Probates. 3rd edition. Consumers' Association and Penguin, London, 1994.

Explains in clear terms how to make a straightforward will and how to administer the estate of someone who has died, without using a solicitor.

Appendix G:
Palliative Care and Hospice Care

'Palliative care is the active, total care of patients whose disease no longer responds to curative treatment, and for whom the goal must be the best quality of life for them and their families.' *The National Council for Hospice and Specialist Palliative Care Services*

Hospice and palliative care are now part of the health care system. There is a wide range of care, from hospice home care through day hospices to full institutional hospices. Like any other specialist service, you can be referred to it by your family doctor or hospital.

The Hospice Information Service offers information and support by telephone. It publishes an excellent free annual *Directory of Hospice Services in the UK and Republic of Ireland*; send an 11 × 9 inch stamped self-addressed envelope to:

The Hospice Information Service, St Christopher's Hospice, 51–59 Lawrie Park Road, Sydenham, London SE26 6DZ. Tel: 0181 778 9252 ext 262/263; Fax: 0181 659 8680.

Appendix H:
Taxation Relief For Donations

Some donations may entitle you to tax relief, if they are made to a registered charitable organisation.

For further information, discuss with a tax consultant or accountant, or write to Inland Revenue Claims, Trusts and Charities, St John's House, Merton Road, Bootle, Merseyside L69 9BB. Tel: 0151 472 6000.

Index

The Women's Press is Britain's leading women's publishing house. Established in 1978, we publish high-quality fiction and non-fiction from outstanding women writers worldwide. Our exciting and diverse list includes literary fiction, detective novels, biography and autobiography, health, women's studies, handbooks, literary criticism, psychology and self help, the arts, our popular Livewire Books for Teenagers young adult series and the bestselling annual *Women Artists Diary* featuring beautiful colour and black-and-white illustrations from the best in contemporary women's art.

If you would like more information about our books, please send an A5 sae for our latest catalogue and complete list to:

The Sales Department
The Women's Press Ltd
34 Great Sutton Street
London EC1V 0DX
Tel: 0171 251 3007
Fax: 0171 608 1938

Stephanie Dowrick
Intimacy and Solitude
Balancing Closeness and Independence

Why is it that when we are in intimate relationships, we
may often feel dissatisfied, inadequate and claustrophobic?
But then, once we are on our own, we get lonely and have
difficulties enjoying solitude? In this internationally bestselling book, Stephanie Dowrick draws on a wide range
of personal experiences, and on psychotherapy's most
useful insights, to show how success in intimacy depends
on success in solitude — and vice versa.

Whether experiencing solitude through choice or through
circumstance, *Intimacy and Solitude* enables us to discover
our own unique inner world — and offers real possibilities
for lasting, positive change.

**'Sympathetically, and with a rare clarity, it offers
penetrating insights into some of the most basic
paradoxes of human relationships.'** *Guardian*

**'Essential reading...A penetrating, thoroughly
researched, thoughtful and thought-provoking
analysis. Don't stay home on your own without it.'**
Mary Scott, *Everywoman*

Self Help/Therapy/Sexual Politics £7.99
ISBN 0 7043 4308 8

Stephanie Dowrick
The Intimacy and Solitude Self-Therapy Book

In this companion volume to her bestselling book, *Intimacy and Solitude*, Stephanie Dowrick guides us towards greater fulfilment and joy through simple, effective self-therapy. She does not provide formula answers, hoping they might fit. Instead, using focused explorations and active meditations, she inspires us to look afresh at our lives, enabling us to strengthen ourselves and to find enrichment and reward in solitude as well as intimacy.

'A treasure trove of exercises...This book should be on any self-respecting bedside table. Read it. Use it. Return to it as you would a familiar friend in times of need.' *Everywoman*

'A very, very good book...It speaks to me; to modern experiences in relationships, much like a profoundly satisfying conversation, late into the evening with a very good friend. Thank you, Stephanie.'
Journal of Interprofessional Care

Self Help/Therapy/Sexual Politics £7.99
ISBN 0 7043 4377 0

The Women's Press Handbook Series

Kathy Nairne and Gerrilyn Smith
Dealing with Depression

Second Edition – Fully revised and updated

Why do so many women suffer from depression? How can
we defend ourselves against this common problem and get
out of what can quickly become a vicious circle?

Kathy Nairne and Gerrilyn Smith, both clinical psychologists,
draw on their extensive professional experience together
with the experiences of a wide range of women sufferers
to offer this down-to-earth and comprehensive guide to
dealing with depression. Identifying the many possible
causes of depression, including bereavement and chronic
illness, the authors also outline the many forms depression
can take. Finally, they explore different ways of coping and
recovering, and evaluate the help available, to offer an
essential handbook for anyone who has experienced
depression, either in themselves or others.

**'A straightforward, practical guide...it explores its
subject in depth.'** *Company*

**'I can thoroughly recommend this practical,
sympathetic and non-patronising book.'**
London Newspaper Group

Health/Self Help £6.99
ISBN 0 7043 4443 2

Also of interest:

Mary Jones
Secret Flowers
Mourning and the Adaptation to Loss

When Mary Jones' husband died of cancer, she found she had to re-experience her love for him in life in order to accept his death. After many years of being secure in the knowledge of their love and life together, she had to learn, suddenly, how to live alone.

Now in this remarkable personal account of bereavement, Mary Jones describes with clarity and candour the different stages of grief and loss: from the realisation that her husband's death was inevitable through to his last days in a hospice, his funeral and her difficult new life afterwards...

'A moving record of bereavement and grief which will comfort all those who have to face the death of someone dear and the pain and isolation that can involve.' *She* magazine

'Full of unexpected insights.' *Cruse News*

'Compulsive reading...Mary Jones has important things to say and she says them clearly, honestly and intricately.' *Bereavement Care*

Autobiography £2.95
ISBN 0 7043 4122 0

Sandra Butler and Barbara Rosenblum
Cancer in Two Voices

'Moving and powerful. A three-year journey shared
by two courageous women. A message shines out
for all of us.' Sheila Kitzinger

Cancer in Two Voices is the remarkable and deeply inspiring
collaboration between Barbara Rosenblum and Sandra
Butler which began when Barbara was diagnosed with
breast cancer. Through journal entries and letters they
share the experience of living with cancer and being the
partner who survives.

Despite all adversities, not least the medical negligence
which contributed to Barbara's death, their dialogue is a
celebration of life's many choices, and an affirmation of the
strength of women's love.

**'The most compelling and memorable document
about cancer I have ever read.'** *Community Care*

Health/Autobiography £6.99
ISBN 0 7043 4393 2